SOCIAL THOUGHT ON ALCOHOLISM

A Comprehensive Review

edited by
Thomas D. Watts
The University of Texas at Arlington

with a Foreword by
Richard L. Rachin
Editor, *Journal of Drug Issues*

ROBERT E. KRIEGER PUBLISHING COMPANY
MALABAR, FLORIDA
1986

Original Edition 1986

Printed and Published by
ROBERT E. KRIEGER PUBLISHING COMPANY, INC.
KRIEGER DRIVE
MALABAR, FLORIDA 32950

Printed in the United States of America

Library of Congress Cataloging-in-Publication Data

Main entry under title:

Social thought on alcoholism.

Includes indexes.
1. Alcoholism—Addresses, essays, lectures.
I.   Watts, Thomas D.
HV5047.S63 1986 362.2'92 85-23921
ISBN 0-89874-925-5

10 9 8 7 6 5 4 3 2

To Mrs. Doris E. Hansen

FOREWORD

Improvement in our understanding of the seemingly endless and multi-faceted issues surrounding alcoholism has been, at best, an incremental and often confusing accomplishment. Divergent hypotheses, theories, and beliefs characterize our knowledge base and are revealing of the complexity of the issues surrounding its nature, etiology, effects, and treatment. When we consider this matter, it would be presumptuous to deny that our understanding of these issues leaves much to be desired. Certainly, those who struggle daily on the front lines confronting alcoholism, witnessing its effects, and correlating its use with a host of social phenomena are well acquainted with our paucity of knowledge.

The *Journal of Drug Issues*, which over the years has striven to provide its readers with an objective and probing focus on some of the more controversial aspects of substance use and abuse, was particularly pleased to include the original collection of articles appearing in this book. Experience with the various theme issues that *JDI* has published over its fifteen-year history, and some that it has not published, has indicated a discernible relationship between the breadth and scope of their inquiry and their keenness and purpose of focus. Much like an optical lens, the challenge to any author increases in proportion to the diversity and range of his or her topic.

Edited collections pose considerable obstacles and challenges. It falls to the editor to weave an organized, integrated whole with articles whose purpose was either never intended as linkages in some topical collection or, if purposely prepared, rarely completed with this as a primary consideration.

Readers of *Social Thought on Alcoholism* will find that its editor and his contributors have responded well to this challenge and have succeeded in accomplishing the purpose for which a well-developed collection achieves value and benefit.

Professor Watts not only makes clear the obvious problems and limitations of organizing a collection devoted to a constantly evolving, developing, and unfolding subject—which indeed is what social thought on any subject of enduring significance would be—but he appropriately reminds the reader that this collection makes no pretense of being more than carefully chosen and well-written selections that simply provide one additional step toward both building and integrating our knowledge.

All the articles save two are included from the original collection. The Clemmons, Saleebey, and Watts articles have been revised from the original. The chapters in this book are written from an interdisciplinary perspective and in a style that will interest both lay and professional readers including students, teachers, researchers, policy makers and practitioners.

The book is organized into three parts: An Overview of Social Thought On Alcoholism, Changing Cultural and Religious Beliefs, and Alcoholics and Social Thought on Alcoholism. Eleven articles constitute the collection. Its contributors have rich and varied backgrounds as researchers, theoreticians, educators, and practitioners. They include sociologists, psychologists, historians, anthropologists, and social workers, possessing a variety and depth of experience with beverage alcohol issues. Together they provide the reader with the integrated contributions of a group with broad perspectives and experience. All have previously contributed extensively to the literature in this field; they join together in this volume to provide the reader with a timely, original, and significant collection.

I am particularly pleased that this excellent addition to our understanding of the complex and often frustrating issues surrounding beverage alcohol will be brought to the attention of a much wider audience than any scholarly journal can ever expect to reach. As a result, it should help realize the hope expressed originally by Professor Watts that this contribution "open some new doors for better understanding the immense problem of alcohol, alcohol abuse, and alcoholism."

Richard L. Rachin
Editor, Journal of Drug Issues

ACKNOWLEDGMENTS

Many people have contributed to this book. Thanks go to all of the authors of the chapters in this book for their sound contributions here to increasing our understanding of social thought on alcoholism. Thanks go to Rita Anderson, Connie Clifton and Carol Davis for their work on the manuscript, to Richard L. Rachin, editor of the *Journal of Drug Issues*, for his continuing assistance and support, to my family for their support, and to anyone else I may not have mentioned here who in any way contributed to assisting in the process of bringing this book to fruition.

"So we must take the whole subject of convivial drinking into fuller consideration; it is a practice of grave importance, and calls for the judgement of no mean legislator. The question is not that of the mere drinking of wine or its complete prohibition, but of the convivial drinking of it. Should we follow the fashion of Scythians and Persians (to say nothing of Carthaginians, Celts, Iberians, and Thracians, who are all of them warlike peoples), or that of your own countrymen? They, as you remind me, absolutely reject the practice, whereas the Scythians and Thracians, men and women alike, take their wine neat, and let it run down over their garments and count this a laudable and glorious practice. The Persians, again, indulge freely in this, as in other luxurious habits which you Spartans prohibit, though with less disorder than the nations I have mentioned."

--Plato* (c. 4238–348/347 B.C.)

*Plato, *The Laws*, Book I, trans. by A. E. Taylor. London: J.M. Dent & Sons, Ltd., 1960, p. 14.

CONTENTS

ix

"THE PARAMETERS OF 'SOCIAL THOUGHT ON ALCOHOLISM': SOME COMMENTS"
Thomas D. Watts

This book focuses on "social thought on alcoholism." It is a subject that is very much before our minds and in our thinking in the current period (Wiener, 1981). Perhaps not since the Prohibition Era have we seen the role of alcohol and society debated with as much intensity in the United States as in the contemporary period. Alcohol advertisements in the mass media, legislation on drunk driving, labeling of alcoholic beverages, and many more issues such as these—important as they all are—are themselves only representative of the "tip of the iceberg" concerning the role of alcohol and society, or social thinking and social thought on alcoholism. This chapter (a) briefly introduces the book and (b) makes a few statements about the possible parameters of the subject of social thought on alcoholism.

Each of the chapters in this book is concerned with some aspect of social thought on alcoholism. There is certainly no pretense here that all aspects of this vast subject expanse are covered, if such an undertaking would even be possible. Part One: "An Overview of Social Thought on Alcoholism" begins with this chapter, followed by a chapter by David A. Ward on the nature and treatment of alcoholism. The third chapter, by Dennis Saleebey, discusses social psychological perspectives on addiction; concluding Part One is the fourth chapter, by Robert T. Tournier, on the sociohistorical origins of, and the degree of acceptance of, the disease conception of alcoholism.

Part Two: "Changing Cultural and Religious Beliefs" begins with Chapter 5 concerning religious views on alcohol and alcoholism, by James E. Royce; followed by Chapter 6, on cultural beliefs and alcohol, by Mac Marshall; Chapter 7, on reflections of social thought in research on women and alcoholism, by Penny Clemmons; Chapter 8, on the pioneering investigations on alcohol and poverty of John James McCook, by David T. Courtwright and Shelby Miller; and Chapter 9, concerning current social thought on alcohol and marijuana, by Barbara Lynn Kail. Part Three: "Alcoholics and Social Thought on Alcoholism" incorporates Chapter 10 on the social thought of alcoholics, by Ernest Kurtz and Linda Farris Kurtz and Chapter 11, on social thought and Alcoholics Anonymous, by Lincoln J. Fry.

Each of the chapters in this book makes its own unique contribution to improving our collective understanding of this complex subject. For further reading, the reader is referred here to other works by each of the authors who have contributed to this book. This book should be looked at as a concerned effort to understand many aspects (but not all aspects) of a vast intellectual, professional, and societal terrain—"social thought on alcoholism."

So vast is this terrain, so extensive are the parameters of social thought on alcoholism that Keller (1976:6) has said quite succinctly that: "In the beginning, there was alcohol." Alcohol and alcoholism have been with us throughout the history of the United States (Howland and Howland, 1978) and, indeed, throughout the history of the human race (Tongue, 1978). Studying the subject of social thought on alcohol and alcoholism (and here, perhaps, social thought on alcohol should be distinguished from social thought on alcoholism) over such a wide expanse of time, of cultures (Heath and Cooper, 1981), civilizations, and belief systems would be a considerable undertaking. Such an undertaking would require a large historial base (perhaps Toynbee's vast, multivolume *A Study of History* (1947, 1957) would provide such a base); so vast is the subject of "alcohol in history".

We have begun our examination of the parameters of social thought on alcoholism with mention of the historical base; following closely behind should be the study of philosophy, philosophy of science, religious thought, and belief systems. Belief systems are located in different cultures; hence, anthropology would be another possible area of study. But let us not stop there: sociology, political science, criminal justice, social work and social welfare, philosophy, theology and religious studies, economics, and a host of other disciplines and professions would be included in our study. The study of the history of the natural and physical sciences would be important here. The natural sciences (biology, etc.) have in recent years given us important new insights into the longstanding question of a possible hereditary or physiological base for alcoholism problems. This in turn contributes to changes in social thought on alcoholism. The criticism in recent years of the disease model of alcoholism (Conrad and Schneider, 1980) may take different directions in the future, with advances in knowledge about the biology of alcoholism.

The parameters of social thought on alcoholism can be initially deciphered by studying social thought itself. Social thought can be defined as the totality of the thinking of human beings about their relationships and obligations to other human beings (Fairchild, 1967:294). Social thought relates or conjoins with the social mores, social values, and social histories of societies. Social history has become more important in recent decades in the field of history in the United States (Tingley, 1979), in Britain (Mitchell, 1979:184), and elsewhere. Attitudes toward alcohol and toward alcoholism are an important part of social history. Indeed, we could say here that attitudes toward both alcohol and alcoholism during given historical periods tell us a lot about the social history of that period (the Prohibition era, for example, so well analyzed by Gusfield (1963) and others).

Social thought on alcoholism is in a noteworthy sense a societal record, a patterning of social mores and values, an important chronicle of cultural and social history (Watts, 1982). Social thought on alcoholism can be looked at as constantly evolving, developing, and unfolding. "Societal learning" (Watts, 1981) can be defined as "the processes by which society gathers and internalizes knowledge about the changing conditions of both its internal and external environment" (Friedmann, 1981:246). Individuals, groups, and societies are engaged in a continual learning process about alcohol and alcoholism. Social thought on alcoholism is not limited to what theoreticians and researchers (such as Benjamin Rush, E.M. Jellinek, Seldon Bacon, Mark Keller, Dan Beauchamp, Stanton Peele, and others) say about alcohol and alcoholism; it extends to what the ordinary citizen thinks and much more. The man or woman on the street is a social thinker and has views on the role that alcohol should play (or not play) in society. Eric Hoffer (1974) was neither an academic nor a social scientist, yet his works were an important contribution to social thought. But to go further, most so-called social thinking on alcohol and alcoholism by people in various cultures or societies probably has gone unrecorded. Given the limitations of most positivist social science methodology (Filmer, Phillipson, Silverman, and Walsh, 1972), it may be difficult or even impossible to uncover the real meanings that many people attach to alcohol and alcoholism. In this sense, it would probably be most helpful to attempt to understand the subject from a phenomenological perspective (Wallace, 1977).

To extend the parameters of social thought on alcoholism further, we must anchor our thinking in specific cultural contexts. Alcohol cannot be looked at outside the cultural locations in which it is consumed (or abused, and our definition of "abuse" must itself be anchored firmly in a cultural context). In the United States, the attitudes and views of people from minority populations toward alcohol and alcoholism have not received much attention until recent decades.

Among Hispanic Americans, there are various cultural beliefs about alcohol and alcoholism (Alcocer, 1982) and about health (Martinez, 1978) and mental health (Padilla and Ruiz, 1973, 1974) that influence Hispanic social thinking about alcoholism. This is true as well concerning Native Americans (Mail and McDonald, 1980). The "firewater myth" concerning Native Americans implies that they are "constitutionally prone to develop an inordinate craving for liquor and to lose control over their behavior when they drink" (Leland, 1971:1). Interestingly, this facet of social thought concerning Native American alcoholism may conceivably serve as a kind of "self-fulfilling prophecy" in some cases. Many younger Indians "grow up with the idea that to drink is to be Indian, and vice versa. The fact that most of the great chiefs of the past—Tecumseh, Crazy Horse, Sitting Bull—were opposed to liquor is not well publicized" (Lewis, 1982:320).

The historical, cultural, and environmental contexts of black alcoholism (Harper, 1976; Watts and Wright, 1983; Wright and Watts, 1985; Watts and Wright, 1986) are important in respect to understanding black social thinking on alcohol and alcoholism. Long before the Europeans reached the African continent, black Africans had established traditions that governed the use of alcohol (National Institute on Alcohol Abuse and Alcoholism, (1981:8). During the slavery period, alcohol was often given to the slaves to keep them quiet and manageable (Larkins, 1965). This was not the first time (or last) for alcohol to be used in such a manner. This external control aspect was well stated by Frederick Douglass (1846 (1979:166)).

On each Saturday night it is quite common in Maryland (the slave state from which I escaped) for masters to give their slaves a considerable quantity of whisky to keep them during the Sabbath in a state of stupidity. At the time when they would be apt to think—at a time when they would be apt to devise means for their freedom—their masters give them of the stupefying draught which paralyzes their intellect, and in this way prevents their seeking emancipation.

Frederick Douglass, W. E. B. DuBois, and other noteworthy representatives of black social thought have warned of the dangers of heavy drinking as a stumbling block on the road to equality (Harvey, 1985:88).

We can and should extend the parameters of social thinking about alcohol and alcoholism to include Asian-American perspectives (Kitano, 1982), and those of all cultures throughout the world (Heath and Cooper, 1981). The attitudes and social thinking of women concerning alcohol and alcoholism (see Chapter 7 by Penny Clemmons) need to be considered, as well as those of low income groups (from whatever race or culture), the mentally handicapped, the physically handicapped (Watts, 1982–83), the aged (Barnes, et al., 1980), and many other populations.

In order to extend the parameters of social thought on alcohol abuse and alcoholism, we must consider methodological approaches to understanding complex social phenomena such as alcohol abuse and alcoholism that can enable us to begin to explicate the *meanings* that people attach to alcohol (which is closely conjoined with social thinking on alcohol). Ethnomethodology (Garfinkel, 1967; Ramos, 1973; Watts, 1985) is an approach that goes beyond participant observation and can aid us considerably in this effort. This does not in any way rule out quantitative approaches. It might be stated that the best methodological approaches here would combine sound qualitative and sound quantitative elements. Indeed, the complexity of the issue of alcohol and alcoholism in society demands appropriate, sophisticated, comprehensive research methodologies with which to approach the subject.

I think I can speak for the authors included here in saying that we hope these contributions will open some new doors for better understanding the immense problem of alcohol, alcohol abuse, and alcoholism. This is neither the complete word nor the last word on the subject. The reader is invited to utilize this source along with other sources in gaining new knowledge about the subject. We do hope that those who explore this subject now and in later years will find this book of much use.

REFERENCES

Alcocer, Anthony M.
1982 "Alcohol Use and Abuse among the Hispanic American Population." *Alcohol and Health Monograph 4: Special Population Issues.* Rockville, Md.: National Institute on Alcohol Abuse and Alcoholism: 361–382.
Barnes, Grace M., Ernest L. Abel, and Charles A. S. Ernst
1980 *Alcohol and the Elderly: A Comprehensive Bibliography.* Westport, Conn.: Greenwood Press.
Conrad, Peter, and Joseph W. Schneider
1980 *Deviance and Medicalization: From Badness to Sickness.* St. Louis, Mo.: C. V. Mosby Co.
Cuzzort, Ray P., and Edith W. King
1980 *Twentieth Century Social Thought.* New York: Holt, Rinehart & Winston.
Douglass, Frederick
1846 "Intemperance Viewed in Connection with Slavery: An Address
(1979) Delivered in Glasgow, Scotland, on 18 February 1846." Reported in the Glasgow *Saturday Post*, 21 February 1846. *The Frederick Douglass Papers, Series One: Speeches, Debates, and Interviews.* Volume 1: 1841–46, ed. by John W. Blassingame. New Haven, Conn.: Yale University Press.
Fairchild, Henry Pratt (ed.)
1967 *Dictionary of Sociology and Related Sciences.* Totowa, N.J.: Littlefield, Adams and Co., Inc.
Filmer, Paul, Michael Phillipson, David Silverman, and David Walsh
1972 *New Directions in Sociological Theory.* Cambridge, Mass.: MIT Press.
Friedmann, John
1981 *Retracking America: A Theory of Transactive Planning.* Emmaus, Pa.: Rodale Press. Reissue of book published originally in 1973 by Anchor Press/Doubleday.
Garfinkel, Harold
1967 *Studies in Ethnomethodology.* Englewood Cliffs, N.J.: Prentice-Hall.
Gusfield, Joseph R.
1963 *Symbolic Crusade: Status Politics and the American Temperance Movement.* Urbana, Ill.: University of Illinois Press.
Harper, Frederick D.
1976 *Alcohol and Blacks: an Overview.* Alexandria, Va.: Douglas Publ.
Harvey, William B.
1985 Alcohol Abuse and the Black Community: A Contemporary Analysis. *Journal of Drug Issues* 15, no. 1 (Winter, 1985): 81–91.

Heath, Dwight B., and A. M. Cooper
   1981   *Alcohol Use and World Cultures: A Comprehensive Bibliography of Anthropological Sources.*   Bibliographic Series No. 15.   Toronto, Ontario, Canada: Addiction Research Foundation.
Hoffer, Eric
   1974   *Reflections on the Human Condition.* New York: Harper and Row.
Howland, Richard B., and Joe W. Howland, M.D.
   1978   200 Years of Drinking in the United States: Evolution of the Disease Concept.   In *Drinking: Alcohol in American Society–Issues and Current Research,* edited by John A. Ewing, M.D., and Beatrice A. Rouse, 39–60. Chicago: Nelson-Hall.
Keller, Mark
   1976   "Problems with Alcohol: An Historical Perspective."   In *Alcohol and Alcohol Problems: New Thinking and New Directions,*   edited by William J. Filstead, Jean J. Rossi, and Mark Keller, 5–28.   Cambridge, Mass.: Ballinger.
Kitano, Harry H. L.
   1982   "Alcohol Drinking Patterns: The Asian Americans."   *Alcohol and Health Monograph 4:   Special Population Issues.*   Rockville, Md.:   National Institute on Alcohol Abuse and Alcoholism: 411–430.
Larkins, John R.
   1965   *Alcohol and the Negro: Explosive Issues.*   Zebulon, N.C.:   Record Publ. Co.
Leland, Joy
   1976   *Firewater Myths: North American Indian Drinking and Alcohol Addiction.* New Brunswick, N.J.: Rutgers Center of Alcohol Studies.
Lewis, Ronald G.
   1982   "Alcoholism and the Native American—A Review of the Literature." *Alcohol and Health Monograph 4:   Special Population Issues.*   Rockville, Md.: National Institute of Alcohol Abuse and Alcoholism: 315–328.
Mail, Patricia D., and David R. McDonald
   1980   *Tulapai to Takay: A Bibliography of Alcohol Use and Abuse Among Native Americans of North America.*   New Haven, Conn.:   Human Relations Area Files Press.
Martinez, Ricardo Arguijo (ed.)
   1978   *Hispanic Culture and Health Care: Fact, Fiction, Folklore.*   St. Louis, Mo.: C. V. Mosby Co.
Mitchell, G. Duncan (ed.)
   1979   *A New Dictionary of the Social Sciences.* New York: Aldine Publ. Co.
National Institute on Alcohol Abuse and Alcoholism
   1981   *A Guidebook for Planning Alcohol Prevention Programs with Black Youth.* Rockville, Md.: National Institute on Alcohol Abuse and Alcoholism.
Padilla, Amado, and Rene A. Ruiz
   1973   *Latino Mental Health: A Review of Literature.*   Rockville, Md.:   National Institute of Mental Health.

1974 *Latino Mental Health: Bibliography and Abstracts.* Rockville, Md.: National Institute of Mental Health.
Ramos, Reyes
A Case in Point: An Ethnomethodological Study of a Poor Mexican American Family. *Social Science Quarterly,* vol. 53, no. 4 (March, 1973): 905–919.
Tingley, Donald F.
1979 *Social History of the United States: A Guide to Information Sources.* Detroit, Mich.: Gale Research Co.
Tongue, Archer
1978 "5,000 Years of Drinking." In *Drinking: Alcohol in American Society – Issues and Current Research,* edited by John A. Ewing, M.D., and Beatrice A. Rouse, 31–38. Chicago: Nelson-Hall.
Toynbee, Arnold J.
1947, *A Study of History.* Abr. ed. Somervell, D.C., ed. Incl. Vols. 1–6.
1957 1947. Vols. 7–10, 1957. New York: Oxford University Press.
Wallace, John
1977 "Alcoholism From the Inside Out: A Phenomenological Analysis." In *Alcoholism: Development, Consequences, and Interventions,* edited by Nada J. Estes and M. Edith Heinemann, 3–14. St. Louis, Mo.: The C. V. Mosby Co.
Watts, Thomas D.
1982–83
Alcoholism and the Disabled, *International Quarterly of Community Health Education* 3, no. 1: 92–97.
Watts, Thomas D.
1985 "Ethnomethodology," Chap. 18. In *Social Work Research and Evaluation,* 2d ed., ed. Richard M. Grinnell, Jr. Itasca, Ill.: F. E. Peacock Publ., Inc.
Watts, Thomas D.
1981 *The Societal Learning Approach: A New Approach to Social Welfare Policy and Planning in America.* Palo Alto and Saratoga, California: Century Twenty One Publ., Div. of R and E Research Assocs.
Watts, Thomas D.
1982 Three Traditions in Social Thought on Alcoholism, *International Journal of the Addictions* 17, no. 7: 1231–1239.
Watts, Thomas D. and Roosevelt Wright, Jr., (eds.)
1986 *Black Alcohol Abuse and Alcoholism: An Annotated Bibliography.* New York: Praeger Publ. Co.
Watts, Thomas D., and Roosevelt Wright, Jr., (eds.)
1983 *Black Alcoholism: Toward a Comprehensive Understanding.* Springfield, Ill.: Charles C. Thomas Publ.
Wiener, Carolyn
1981 *The Politics of Alcoholism: Building an Arena Around a Social Problem.* New Brunswick, N.J.: Transaction Books.

Wright, Roosevelt, Jr., and Thomas D. Watts, (eds.)
    1985 *Prevention of Black Alcoholism: Issues and Strategies.*   Springfield, Ill.:
          Charles C. Thomas Publ.

CONCEPTIONS OF THE NATURE AND TREATMENT OF ALCOHOLISM

David A. Ward

This paper provides an analytical comparison of seven current conceptions of alcoholism. Six dimensions are used for the purposes of comparison: (1) definition of alcoholism; (2) etiology; (3) alcoholic personality; (4) epidemiology; (5) treatment; and (6) prognosis. In addition to the traditional conceptions of alcoholism such as AA and family therapy, the paper examines three more recent points of view—namely, the behavioral, the sociological, and the transactional conceptions. Throughout the analysis, areas of disagreement are highlighted and important issues arising from these disagreements underscored.

In the field of alcoholism theory and treatment, a number of conceptual frameworks have been advanced, each of which purports to explain the nature of alcoholism better than the others. One approach might define alcoholism as a disease while another might argue that alcoholism is a bad habit resulting from lack of will power. Since we have not been able to provide adequate evidence as to which conception is most valid, the way one approaches alcoholism is often a matter of individual preference. At various times in history, one conception will be more popular than another. Over time, some views will fall into relative disrepute, often giving way to a new (and we hope, more scientifically defensible) theoretical approach. Currently there exist in the field of alcoholism theory and treatment about eight or ten different theoretical approaches to alcoholism. Some are totally opposite in their definition of alcoholism, their theory regarding etiology, and their prescription for treatment. Others, however, are fairly similar, having only shades of difference. In this paper, we will examine some of the important theoretical models that are currently used in the field. We asked questions regarding the way a particular model addresses such issues as the definition of alcoholism, its etiology, and its treatment. Each of these questions can be considered dimensions in which the various conceptions might be compared. With these and other dimensions in mind, seven different theoretical approaches currently in use in varying degrees are examined. Siegler, Osmond, and Newell (1968) were the first to provide such an analysis, but they omit three recent models which have received a good deal of attention—namely, the behavioral model, the sociological model, and the

David A. Ward is Associate Professor of Sociology in the Department of Sociology at Washington State University, Pullman, Washington. He received his Ph.D. at the University of Florida in 1975, whereupon he accepted the position of Director of the Alcoholism Studies Program at Washington State. His research and writings in the field of alcoholism include his introductory textbook entitled *Alcoholism: Introduction to Theory and Treatment*, a number of articles in a wide range of journals, including *Journal of Marriage and the Family*, *Journal of Health and Social Behavior*, *Journal of Drug Issues*, and *International Journal of the Addictions*, and a guest edition for *Journal of Drug Issues* entitled "The Use of Legal and Non-Legal Coercion in the Prevention and Treatment of Alcohol and Drug Abuse." His current research focuses on the relationship between alcohol abuse and criminal behavior.

transactional approach. Therefore, the present paper, by including them, may be considered more comprehensive.

Alcoholics Anonymous Conception

Alcoholics Anonymous is one of the oldest and most successful treatment programs for alcoholics. Begun over forty years ago by two men who were alcoholics themselves, AA now has a membership estimated at approximately 50,000. It is fair to say that the AA model is the most popular conception of alcoholism and its treatment in current use.

1. Definition

The AA model defines alcoholism as a disease. The term *disease* usually has two separate but related meanings. First, the alcoholic has a disease of the body. Either due to some inherited predisposition or to a changed physiological response resulting from long years of drinking, the alcoholic's body is affected differently by alcohol. Second, the alcoholic has a disease of the mind—an obsession with alcohol and its effects. This second definition of disease is often related to a spiritual failing. The earmark of alcoholism according to the AA model is loss of control over one's drinking. Physiological addiction and loss of control are the essence of the disease, alcoholism.

2. Etiology

It is not overly simplistic to say that the cause of alcoholism, according to the AA model, is drinking alcohol. The reason that some people can drink and not become alcoholic while others do is because the alcoholic is different emotionally and/or spiritually as well as physically. Stated differently, the potential alcoholic is both psychologically and biologically susceptible to becoming an alcoholic. Drinking brings out this susceptibility in the alcoholic, but not in the normal social drinker. Though the precise, physiological factors responsible for the alcoholic's susceptibility are not scientifically known, the proponents of the AA model point to the fact that different people can drink similar amounts of alcohol over the same length of time and only some develop alcoholism. This is at least indirect evidence that the true alcoholic is constitutionally different and that this difference may be an inherited physiological susceptibility.

3. Alcoholic Personality

Those who subscribe to the Alcoholics Anonymous model would argue that similarities in personality configurations among alcoholics are consequences rather than causes of the alcoholic condition. Since alcoholism according to the AA conception is caused by inherited physiological factors, any psychological abnormalities such as paranoia, low self-esteem, depression, and the like are not causal determinants of the alcoholic disease condition, but are either concomitants to or resultants of the uncontrollable drinking behavior. Hence, the AA model would come down on the side of what Barnes (1979) has called the "clinical" alcoholic personalty.

4. Epidemiology

The empirical relationship between social class position and problem drinking presents somewhat of a problem for the AA model. If alcoholism is inherited as the AA view holds, then either lower class persons are genetically inferior (or at least genetically different) than persons in the upper classes, or true alcoholic drinking is evenly distributed across social classes, which is an assertion inconsistent with known epidemiologic findings. The only tenable position to be held by the proponents of the AA model is that the relationship between social class and alcoholism is due to "drift." That is, rather than lower class status leading to alcoholism, it is alcoholic drinking that results in lower class status. While this position is at least theoretically defensible, the bulk of the empirical data is not particularly supportive of this hypothesis.

5. Treatment

The treatment program of Alcoholics Anonymous consists of joining together with other alcoholics to help each other stay sober. This process consists of periodic meetings in which the members of the group work through the well-known "12 steps." Also, it is typical for one who is just beginning the recovery process to have a sponsor. The sponsor is an AA member, often with years of sobriety, who helps the newly recovering alcoholic during times of difficulty. Suffice it to say now that AA is one of the most popular and successful treatment programs known.

A noticeable aspect of the AA model, which stems from the definition of alcoholism and the statements regarding etiology, is the insistence upon complete abstinence in the recovery process. Proponents of this model would argue that a true alcoholic can never be cured in the sense of returning to normal social drinking since the alcoholic is constitutionally different. Therefore, the only way to successfully deal with alcoholism is to stop drinking entirely. This aspect of the AA program has resulted in a good deal of controversy within the field of alcoholism treatment and will be highlighted when we examine the behavioral model in later pages.

6. Prognosis

The proponents of the AA model would argue that the likelihood of successful treatment (the prognosis) for those who follow the AA program is very good. They would point to the half million estimated members of AA as ample evidence of the program's success. Failures, the proponents would argue, are those who did not follow the entire program. Since the program is by definition anonymous, valid scientific evaluation of treatment approach is almost impossible. However, the program has been successful for many alcoholics and is used extensively by a wide range of treatment agencies in addition to the traditional AA group meetings.

Psychoanalytic Conception

Discussions of alcoholism and its treatment appeared in the psychoanalytic literature as far back as 1915 (Cahn, 1970). Later, more systematic statements began to emerge. Dr. Sander Ferenczi (1916), for instance, developed the thesis that alcoholism was an overt manifestation of latent homosexuality. Though much of the early theorizing about alcoholism from this perspective has been largely abandoned, we include the model in this paper because a number of the concepts are still employed by alcoholism therapists today.

1. Definition

Alcoholism, as seen from the perspective of the psychoanalytic model, is a symptom of some underlying personality disorder. Unlike the AA model, which emphasizes physiological dependence, proponents of the psychoanalytic model would argue that if the underlying personality dysfunction is resolved, the alcoholic drinking would disappear.

2. Etiology

The classical psychoanalytic model places heavy emphasis on unconscious motivation in human behavior. Those who adhere to this model would argue that alcoholism is the consequence of an unresolved psychological conflict which has been repressed into the unconscious. Often this unconscious conflict has its roots in early childhood. If, for example, one experiences a traumatic event during the oral stage of psychosexual development, a fixation in that stage may occur. This fixation continues through adulthood if it is not resolved. Excessive drinking is often taken as an indication of one's fixation in the oral stage of psychosexual development.

Another interesting theory concerning the etiology of alcoholism stemming from this model is the idea that alcoholism is chronic suicide. The reasoning is that since there is such a high incidence of suicide among alcoholics, the alcoholic is a suicidal person. But, since he does not want to face up to taking his life, he does it slowly by drinking himself to death. The reason for wanting to commit suicide is some unconscious conflict which is probably rooted in the distant past. If this conflict is not resolved, both alcoholism and suicidal tendencies will persist.

3. Alcoholic Personality

It should be clear, given the etiologic theory of the psychoanalytic model, that alcoholism results from various pre-alcoholic personality types. It has been theorized that frustrations during the oral stage of psychosexual development lead to a personality type that is oral dependent (Bertrand and Masling, 1969). Machover, Russo, Machover, and Plumeau (1959) have advanced the hypothesis that some alcoholics engage in excessive alcohol use as a manifestation of latent homosexual tendencies, and Menninger (1963) has argued that alcoholism is a result of suicidal intentions. The difficulty with these hypotheses is in empirically identifying unconscious motivations that are alleged to cause the alcoholic condition. While some attempts in this regard have been made, psychoanalytic theory remains highly speculative, with most supportive evidence being ex post facto.

4. Epidemiology (Alcoholism and Social Class)

It would seem that psychoanalytic theory would have little to say regarding the relationship between alcoholism and social class. However, one reasonable inference from the model can be drawn that bears at least indirectly on the alcoholism/class relationship. It can be argued with some empirical justification that childrearing varies with social class position and that lower class parents tend to use practices that may produce personality patterns most likely to result in problem drinking behavior. Indeed, research has shown that such personality variables as psychopathic deviance, paranoia, and generalized anxiety are linked to lower class status and also to family environment. Moreover, these personality dimensions have been found to be implicated in alcoholic drinking behavior (Hoffman, 1970). While the psychoanalytic model is not well suited for explaining the class/alcoholism relationship, at least the model is not entirely inconsistent with the finding.

5. Treatment

Since the proponents of this model argue that alcoholism is the result of unconscious conflict which often has its origin in early childhood experiences, the treatment for alcoholism is necessarily long and drawn out. Typically, the analyst will employ two techniques to uncover the underlying personality conflict. First, the free association technique, in which the client reveals the first thing that comes to mind when the analyst presents him with a somewhat ambiguous stimulus (such as a nonsense word), is used in hopes of tapping unconscious (and potentially destructive) thoughts and inner emotional conflicts. The theory is that if these inner thoughts and conflicts are made manifest and "worked through," the client will experience less inner tension and consequently less need to drink excessively. The second technique employed by the analyst is dream analysis. The analyst attempts to make unconscious motivations evident by analyzing dream materials and what they might symbolize. Dream symbolisms, the proponents would contend, are indications of certain unconscious fears, anxieties, and deep inner conflicts which must be worked through consciously if they are to be resolved. It is only by making them evident and working through them that the alcoholic might be helped.

Though this brief discussion of the treatment of alcoholism from the perspective of the psychoanalytic model is necessarily superficial given restrictions of space, it does highlight the model's emphasis on resolving unconscious inner psychological conflicts in the therapeutic process.

6. *Prognosis*

The prognosis for this type of treatment for the alcoholic client is usually poor. It is very time-consuming and requires a person who is trained extensively in psychoanalysis to employ it. Since it is a very lengthy process, the progressive alcoholic drinking often compounds things to the point where real "breakthroughs" are rendered close to impossible.

Medical Model Conception

Whereas proponents of the psychoanalytic model would contend that alcoholism is merely an overt symptom of underlying personality dysfunction, those who adhere to the medical model argue that alcoholism is a manifest symptom of an underlying biochemical disorder. The underlying cause of alcoholism is not psychological but physiological.

1. *Definition*

Alcoholism is a progressive disease having physiological determinants. Alcoholics are people whose body chemistry makes them susceptible to becoming addicted to alcohol. This physiological susceptibility may be inherited.

2. *Etiology*

There are at least two explanations of etiology emanating from the medical model. The first is that certain people are born with a body chemistry that makes them potential alcoholics. When these people begin to drink, the interaction of alcohol with the susceptible physiological makeup results in the symptoms of alcoholism. The second explanation is that long years of drinking may alter the biochemistry of some people, which in turn causes further excessive and uncontrollable drinking characteristic of alcoholism. Though there are differences between these explanations in terms of the initial cause of alcoholism (whether susceptible body chemistry precedes alcoholic drinking or whether excessive drinking precedes altered body chemistry), the final result is the same—alcoholic drinking having a physiological basis.

3. Alcoholic Personality

The view of the alcoholic personality held by the medical model is similar to that of the AA model. The heavy emphasis on physiological determinants of alcoholism dictates that the casual status of personality dysfunctions be posterior to alcoholic drinking behavior.

4. Epidemiology (Alcoholism and Social Class)

Again, the medical model is similar to the AA model when it comes to explaining the relationship between social class position and problem drinking behavior. Alcoholics are hypothesized to take the "Geographic Curve" (Trice, 1962) resulting in a lowering of social status rather than lower class status leading to problem drinking behavior.

5. Treatment

Based on the definition and etiology of alcoholism proposed by adherents of the medical model, you may have observed noticeable similarities between this model and the Alcoholics Anonymous model. In fact, however, there are also important differences. The clinician employing the medical model would, like the AA therapist, attempt to help the alcoholic achieve sobriety or total abstinence, but he might be inclined to use certain minor tranquilizers to ease the pain of withdrawal from alcohol. The AA therapist would argue that even though this might appear humane, the possible result is an addiction to alcohol and another drug. The AA therapist would choose to use social supports such as AA meetings in place of another drug to help in the different times of withdrawal. The therapeutic process for AA is totally drug free. Additionally, the AA therapist emphasizes the spiritual shortcomings of the alcoholic and attempts to help the recovering alcoholic achieve a better relationship with God, "however you define Him."

The relative merits of these respective treatment approaches are left for the student of alcoholism and its treatment to assess. There are certainly positive features in all of the approaches. At the clinical level, the idea would be to combine the positive aspects of all of the models into an effective and successful treatment program.

6. Prognosis

The prognosis for the alcoholic, based on the medical model, is poor. Typically, the medical practitioner is not eager to engage in any type of psychotherapy which would extend beyond a strictly medical approach. Though alcoholism has important physiological causes, it appears that one cannot overlook both psychological and social variables in the recovery process.

Family Interaction Conception
Of the models discussed thus far, only the AA model emphasized the importance of social relationships in the treatment of alcoholism. The family interaction model places sole importance on the alcoholic's relationships with others (particularly family relations) in answering questions about etiology, treatment, and prognosis.

1. Definition
Alcoholism is defined as a family illness. Just as the alcoholic engages in self-destructive and harmful alcoholic drinking, other family members are caught in the web of self-destructive and mutually reinforcing pathological behaviors. Both the alcoholic and the other family members need to be treated.

2. Etiology
Since the relationship between the alcoholic and other family members is seen as circular and mutually reinforcing, it is difficult to pinpoint the original cause of alcoholism. Once the alcoholic process has begun, however, one is able to identify the specific roles each family member plays in sustaining and perpetuating the illness. Roles such as the disgraced parents, the self-pitying spouse, and the neglected children are often apparent to the trained observer. Attempts to change the roles therapeutically often meet with a good deal of resistance, signifying the functions the respective roles serve both for the individual members and the family as a whole.

3. Alcoholic Personality
The family interaction model is most directly applicable for explaining the development of personalities among children of alcoholic families that result in adult problem drinking behavior. Fine (1975) has shown that the personalities and behavioral patterns of children of alcoholic families differ significantly from the personalities of children of nonalcoholic families. Inconsistent childrearing, insecurity, and undue responsibilities for family stability are all characteristic of children of alcoholic families. These family characteristics often result in low self-esteem, anxiety, and inordinate guilt among children of families of alcoholics, which could possibly result in the abuse of alcohol in adulthood. Hence, the correlation between alcohol abuse in adulthood and certain personality dimensions may result from the intrafamilial dynamics typical of alcoholic families in early childhood. Indeed, this explanation is consistent with the finding that alcoholism runs in families, even though most interpret the finding to be evidence for a genetic influence.

4. Epidemiology (Alcoholism and Social Class)
Lower class families are hypothesized to experience greater stresses than

families occupying higher social status. Consistent with a sociological conception, these stresses may instigate heavy alcohol use among family members responsible for the general welfare of the family. Moreover, to the extent that alcoholism is an intergenerational phenomenon, a disproportionate amount of problem drinking among lower class families may lead to problem drinking among offspring, who are likely to occupy a similar social class standing through the dynamics outlined under the alcoholic personality discussion above.

5. Treatment
From the perspective of the family interaction model, the only effective treatment must encompass the whole family. Either this can take the form of counseling the individual members separately or in a conjoint family therapy setting where the entire family participates. Techniques such as confrontation, role playing and/or role reversal are often used. The goal is to help each family member recognize the degree to which they contribute to the circular and degenerative alcoholic process. It is not often recognized, for instance, that bailing the drunk out of jail time after time is merely reinforcing the alcoholic condition though it might give the appearance of love and concern. The therapist will attempt to teach family members alternative behavioral responses which may help break the degenerative feedback process that sustains the alcoholic condition.

6. Prognosis
Proponents of the family interaction model would contend that individual treatment which excludes the other family members is necessarily futile. However, a treatment approach involving the entire family has a high probability of success.

Behavioral Conception
The behavioral model of alcoholism and its treatment is based on a set of principles stemming from behavioral psychology. It is often considered the antithesis of the Alcoholics Anonymous model, setting the stage for considerable controversy and debate in the field.

1. Definition
The behaviorist is reluctant to use the term *alcoholic* because it has disease connotations. Rather, the behaviorist would prefer to speak of drinking behavior that results in problems with living or, more simply, problem drinking. The reason is that the behaviorist does not conceive of alcoholism (if we are permitted to use the term) as being caused by physiological factors such as an inherited biochemical susceptibility, but would contend that factors outside the person (environmental factors) like rewards for heavy drinking, cause problem drinking. This general denial that alcoholism is a disease has created a good deal of

controversy in the field of alcoholism and its treatment.

2. *Etiology*

Behaviorists (and we confine our discussion here to operant behaviorists) are less interested in the original cause of a person's heavy drinking than those factors that sustain it. Heavy or problem drinking is sustained because it is reinforced. A reinforcer is anything that increases the probability of the problem drinking occurring in the future. Events like social approval from peers are important reinforcers that perpetuate problem drinking. Heavy alcohol use can also be maintained by negative reinforcers. When heavy drinking continues because it removes unwanted experiences like anxiety, the heavy drinking is being negatively reinforced. The use of the term *negative* refers to the fact that heavy drinking does away with (negates) anxiety. Nevertheless, the problem drinking is being reinforced since its probability of future occurrence is increased. In general, problem drinking is instigated and maintained by a combination of positive and negative reinforcers.

3. *Alcoholic Personality*

Behavioral psychologists tend not to think of individuals as having personalities in the cognitive sense. Indeed, similar behavioral patterns, such as alcohol abuse, do not arise from common underlying personalities but from factors lying outside the individual, such as similarities in reinforcement history. Therefore, if alcoholics seem to present similar "personality" profiles in the clinical setting it is not that they share inner psychological predispositions but that they merely manifest common behavioral styles resulting from similar reinforcement histories.

4. *Epidemiology (Alcoholism and Social Class)*

Just as reinforcers sustain problem drinking, punishers should stop it. A punisher is any event that decreases the probability of problem drinking occurring in the future. A traumatic experience immediately following a drinking episode and disapproval from significant others are examples of punishers. Just as there are negative reinforcers, there are negative punishers. When something is taken away from a person shortly following heavy drinking, which causes a decrease in drinking, it is called a negative punisher. If previously heavy drinking is decreased by loss of one's driver's license, the lost license is referred to as a negative punisher. A combination of positive and negative punishers should, in theory, curb problem drinking behavior.

6. *Prognosis*

There have been a number of scientific evaluations of the behavioral model in the treatment of alcoholism and, like the other models discussed in this paper, the results have been mixed. One of the largest controversies coming out of the research evaluations of behavioral treatment surrounds the assertion that at least some alcoholics may be able to return to normal drinking. Since the data that bear on this assertion are incomplete, it is difficult to assess the scientific validity of this claim.

Sociological Conception

The models reviewed thus far have focused, for the most part, on individual behavior. They have provided differing ideas about the etiology and treatment of alcoholism that can be applied to particular people. Questions like "Why is *John* an alcoholic, but not his friend?" are questions they are designed to answer. The sociological model shifts the level of inquiry to larger segments of society. Rather than explaining differences in individual drinking behavior, the sociological model is more appropriate for explaining gross differences in alcoholism between social classes or between ethnic groups or religions. Though not exclusively, the sociologist is interested in differences in rates of alcoholism between and within various social categories in society.

1. Definition

Within the sociological model, at least two different perspectives are employed when addressing the problem of alcoholism. The first, or strain perspective, would define alcoholism as a form of deviant behavior. To the degree that drinking behavior exceeds the established norms of the community, it is considered deviant. The second, or labeling perspective, would argue that alcoholism is a label affixed to some people by others (Becker, 1963). This perspective is less concerned with the actual drinking behavior of the person being labeled than it is with the process involved in selecting from the total population of heavy drinkers certain individuals who will be designated as alcoholic. Often these designations are arbitrary and have less to do with how a person drinks than with his social standing in the community. Characteristics such as social class, race, sex, age, and mode of dress often determine whether or not a person will be labeled alcoholic. This is so, irrespective of the person's actual drinking pattern.

2. Etiology

The strain theorist would see alcoholism as a result of an imbalance in the social structure. Merton (1938) has provided one of the most popular expositions of this thesis. He theorizes that, at least in American society, there are a set of common goals toward which everyone in society aspires. Material wealth such as a nice home, a good car, and expensive clothes are examples of common goals toward which Americans aspire. Even though everyone wants these things, not everyone has an equal opportunity to achieve them. Due to artificial barriers like race discrimination in education and employment, certain segments of society (mostly racial and ethnic minorities) are systematically excluded from legitimate opportunities to achieve societal goals. Such opportunity blockage creates a condition of social-structural strain. This imbalance between wanted goals and lack of opportunity creates a sense of hopelessness and helplessness. Alcoholic drinking may provide a means of escape from this unsatisfactory life condition. According to the theory, the lower classes experience a greater degree of blocked opportunity and hence should account for a disproportionate amount of the alcoholic drinking.

As mentioned, the labeling theorist is less interested in the original cause of a person's problem drinking than with what others decide to do about it. However, once the label of alcoholic is attached to someone, the labeling theorist becomes interested in the consequences of that label. Stated another way, the labeling theorist would argue that the "disease label may have disease consequences" (Roman and Trice, 1968). This is not to deny a possible pharmacological basis for alcoholism, but to assign the sick role to someone who is not physically addicted may very well create a self-fulfilling prophecy. This occurs because the sick role assignment (labeling a person alcoholic) absolves the person of responsibility for his drinking behavior. If a person no longer feels responsible (under control) for his drinking, the tendency is to become the very thing he is labeled. The labeling theorist would argue that to label a person alcoholic (even if you are trying to help) may very well create the thing you are trying to prevent. This position stands, of course, directly opposite to the Alcoholics Anonymous model and has created a good deal of controversy in the field.

3. Alcoholic Personality

The issue of the "alcoholic personality" is less germane to strain theory but one directly addressable from the labeling point of view. To the extent that alcoholic labels result in increased problem drinking, they do so through the mediating variable of altered self-conceptions. The assignment of the sick role through labeling transforms the drinker's self-identity into one of a diseased person. It is this fundamental conception of self, then, that perpetuates the alcoholic condition.

4. Epidemiology (Alcoholism and Social Class)

Both the strain theorist and the labeling theorist offer explanations of the social class/alcoholism relationship. The strain theorist argues that lower class individuals experience greater degrees of opportunity blockage which results in frustrations that may lead to problem drinking behavior. The labeling theorist would hold that lower class individuals are more likely to be labeled alcoholic by agents of social control such as mental health workers and alcoholism counselors. These labels, through altered self-conceptions, may lead to a greater incidence of problem drinking among individuals in the lower social classes.

5. Treatment

At one level of analysis, the sociologist would argue that treatment must involve a change in the social structure. Since it is opportunity blockage (following strain theory) that creates a sense of hopelessness often resulting in escapist drinking, the only way to deal with the problem is to ensure equal opportunity to achieve success goals for all segments of society. To treat the individual alcoholic in the clinical setting and then return him to the same disadvantaged life condition is necessarily futile. It is similar to incarcerating the criminal in the name of rehabilitation and then releasing him to return to the same social and economic circumstances that got him to prison in the first place. Since changing the social structure is not within the power of the alcoholism therapist, a less dramatic strategy is suggested. The therapist can help build what Wiseman (1970) has called "social margin." One aspect of social margin involves helping the recovering alcoholic gain important social goals like a marketable job and education, which, when combined with therapy for the drinking problem specifically, will help militate against the hopelessness that instigated the alcoholic condition in the first place.

In addition to the treatment directives deriving from the strain perspective, there are treatment implications stemming from the labeling paradigm. Since it is contended that insidious labeling may very well perpetuate the alcoholic condition through the sick role assignment, the labeling theorist would argue against labeling anyone an alcoholic. It is particularly deleterious to label as alcoholic those who show no signs of physical dependence, since these people still drink under their own volition. This way, the responsibility for changing one's problem drinking remains squarely on the shoulders of the client, thereby preventing unhealthy rationalizing which hinders the therapeutic process significantly.

6. Prognosis

For the sociologist, the likelihood of success in treating alcoholism depends on therapeutic efforts which result in the alcoholic's reentry into the mainstream of social and economic society. Without this social margin, efforts to deal strictly with the drinking behavior will fail. Indeed, the sociologist would point to the success rates of the average treatment program, which show that those who are considered successful are disproportionately middle class clients who are married and gainfully employed.

Transactional Analysis Conception

The transactional approach to understanding human behavior was popularized by Eric Berne in his book entitled *Games People Play*. Later, Claude Steiner became the leader in applying basic concepts of transactional analysis to the understanding and treatment of alcoholism. His article entitled "The Alcoholic Game" (Steiner, 1969) is considered requisite reading for all subscribers to the T.A. approach to alcoholism theory and therapy.

1. Definition

The transactional analyst defines alcoholism as a game rather than a disease. In fact, it is argued that physiological addiction is somewhat inconsequential in the maintenance of alcoholic drinking. Rather, heavy alcohol use is sustained merely because it results in social reinforcers (Strokes) conferred on the alcoholic by those engaged in the alcoholic's network of interpersonal relationships.

2. Etiology

As implied by the definition of alcoholism, the source of alcoholic behavior is not to be found in biochemical factors but in interpersonal transactions. To this degree, the theory of etiology bears similarities to the behavioral approach. The T.A. therapist holds that alcoholics begin with fundamental life scripts which are dominant conceptions of self. They attempt to validate these identities by getting others to participate in interpersonal transactions (games) that serve to reaffirm the initial self-conceptions. As it applies to alcoholism, an individual's script might be "I'm not a worthy person," and its corollary, "neither is anyone else." The interpersonal game might involve the alcoholic's attempt to expose and discredit others who may think they are okay. He will attempt to entice them into one of the alcoholic roles. Roles such as the powerless Rescuer, the Patsy, or just another alcoholic serve to "stroke" the alcoholic and keep the game going.

3. Alcoholic Personality

While it is true that alcoholic behavior has its source in interpersonal relationships, it is also held that certain self-conceptions (scripts) are probably more likely to choose alcoholism as a game. The most dramatic script typical of alcoholics is "I will drink myself to death." But there are other, less dramatic, scripts which are equally typical of alcoholics such as "I am no good."

4. Epidemiology (Alcoholism and Social Class)

There is no systematic statement contained in transactional theory that is particularly fruitful in an attempt to explain the relationship between social class position and alcoholism. Put another way, there is no theoretical reason to believe that alcoholic games should be less prevalent in the middle and upper classes.

5. Treatment

The transactional analyst employs at least three important therapeutic strategies in order to combat the destructive cycle of the alcoholic's game. First, the therapist refuses to participate in the game. This refusal leaves the alcoholic without a motivation to play. Second, the therapist charges the alcoholic with sole responsibility for his alcoholic behavior. The strategy is to preclude the use of rationalizations like scapegoating which impede the therapeutic process and permit the continuation of the game. Third, there is an attempt to create a sense of hope and positive thinking in the alcoholic.

6. Prognosis

Steiner (1969) reports substantial success with the T.A. approach. To the extent that T.A. therapists are drawing on behavioral principles in the treatment process, we should expect similar successes as would be predicted for the behavioral approach to treatment.

Conclusion

In this paper, we have reviewed seven current conceptualizations of alcoholism. The six questions we asked concerning the definition of alcoholism, its etiology, its treatment, and so on have served as points of comparison between the models. We observed similarities between the AA model and the medical model, with their emphasis on physiological factors in the etiology of alcoholism. They did differ in that the AA model sees alcoholism as a spiritual as well as a physical disease. Both of these models differed from the psychoanalytic model in denying that unconscious conflicts are the causes of alcoholism. The behavioral model is contrasted with all three by denying that alcoholism is a physical disease or the result of unconscious motivation. The most controversy in the field of alcoholism theory and treatment surrounds the debate over whether alcoholism is a disease. The behaviorists contend that it isn't, while the proponents of the AA model strongly assert that it is. The family interaction model and the sociological model are not necessarily antagonistic to any of the other models reviewed, although the labeling perspective within the general sociological model would be considered at odds with the disease conception as held by the Alcoholics Anonymous model.

NOTES

1.   While epidemiologic research spans far beyond a mere concern with social class and its relationship to alcoholism, the correlation between class and problem drinking behavior appears to be a major (and indeed invariant) finding from the wealth of studies conducted. Hence, we focus on this variable because it would seem that any theoretical model must at least be consistent with this somewhat unambiguous generalization.

REFERENCES

Becker, H. S.
1963 *Outsiders.* Free Press, a Division of Macmillan Publishing Co.
Barnes, Gordon E.
1979 The Alcoholic Personality. *Journal of Studies on Alcohol* 40:571-634.
Bertrand, S., and J. Masling
1969 Oral Imagery and Alcoholism. *Journal of Abnormal Psychology* 74:50-53.
Cahn, Sidney
1970 *The Treatment of Alcoholics.* New York: Oxford University Press.
Ferenczi, S.
1916 *Contributions to Psychoanalysis.* Boston: Richard Badger.
Fine, E.
1975 *Observations of Young Children From Alcoholic Homes.* West Philadelphia
     Community Mental Health Consortium.
Hoffman, H.
1970 Personality Characteristics of Alcoholics. *Psychological Reports* 27:167-
     171.
Machover, S., F. Russo, K. Machover, and F. Plumeau
1959 An Objective Study of Homosexuality in Alcoholism. *Quarterly Journal of
     Studies on Alcoholism* 20:528-542.
Menninger, K.
1963 *The Vital Balance.* New York: Viking Press.
Merton, R. K.
1938 Social Structure and Anomie. *American Sociological Review* 3:672-682.
Roman, P., and H. Trice
1968 The Sick Role, Labeling Theory and the Deviant Drinker. *International
     Journal of Social Psychiatry* 14:245-251.
Siegler, M., H. Osmond, and S. Newell
1968 Models of Alcoholism. *Quarterly Journal of Alcohol Studies* 29:571-591.
Steiner, C.
1969 The Alcoholic Game. *Quarterly Journal of Studies on Alcohol* 30:920-938.
Trice, H. M.
1962 *Alcoholism in America.* New York: McGraw Hill.
Wiseman, J.
1970 *Stations of the Lost.* Englewood Cliffs, N.J.: Prentice-Hall.

A SOCIAL PSYCHOLOGICAL PERSPECTIVE ON ADDICTION: THEMES AND DISHARMONIES

Dennis Saleebey

It is the thesis of this paper that there is a palpable, perhaps even useful, social psychological theory of addiction now emerging. The basic themes of the evolving theory are reviewed and contrasted with the current "disease" model. However, there are difficulties to be encountered with such a social psychological perspective, and some of these are discussed as well.

Lacking expertise on alcohol and other addictions is, in one sense, a liability. But it does afford a unique opportunity to survey the field with some dispassion and ideological distance. The core of this essay will describe some emerging, though antic, themes—generally social-psychological—on the nature of addiction and briefly sound out some discordant notes as well. Sources for the laying out of these themes are several and include: symbolic interaction theory, "labeling"/ signification theory; McClelland's Power motivation theory and research; the views of Philip Slater on addiction to wealth and Stanton Peele on love and addiction; the theory developing around "controlled drinking"; and radical psychoanalytic theory.

The Themes

1. *Addiction is a species of consciousness, a kind of subjective experience, embellished or dampened by interactional, cultural, and sociopolitical processes and structures.*

This theme becomes somewhat more resonant when its counterpoint, the disease theory of alcoholism, is played. E. M. Jellinek, widely regarded as the sire of the disease concept of alcoholism (or condemned as such), suggested as early as 1946 that alcoholics were "sick" (Jellinek, 1946) and by 1960 had identified five species of alcoholismic drinking, two of which, Gamma and Delta, he labeled as disease (Jellinek, 1960). Roughly characterized, the gamma drinker is the binge drinker, and the delta drinker, though somewhat more moderate, drinks continually, persistently, and increasingly. Jellinek defined both as "sick" drinking because each type evidenced physical dependence and was subject to bouts of "loss of control" drinking (Jellinek, 1960). As it has evolved, the disease concept seems to have several principal components (there is, of course, disagreement over these).

Dennis Saleebey, D.S.W., is Professor of Social Work at the Graduate School of Social Work, The University of Texas at Arlington. He has taught the range of Human Behavior courses at that institution for twelve years, with particular emphasis on mental health, deviance, and social psychological theory. After receiving his doctorate from the University of California at Berkeley, he directed the undergraduate social welfare program at the University of Maine. Professor Saleebey has clinical experience in child guidance, and family and marital counseling.

The alcoholic drinker differs *essentially* from the nonalcoholic drinker. A radical *discontinuity* exists between alcoholismic drinking and any other "type" (social, heavy, even problem drinking). The difference ultimately manifests itself in loss of control drinking, psychophysical dependence, and progressive deterioration of general health. Such a difference can be traced, most likely, to a congenital disorder that produces biochemical dysfunctions so that the alcoholic experiences an atypical physiological reaction to ethanol ingestion—a reaction often typified as an allergic one. The allergy creates the widely noted "craving" syndrome. Given all this, the alcoholic drinker is, in the end, powerless to control his or her drinking and, left untreated, faces the prospect of rapid debilitation on many fronts (Pattison, 1976; Pattison, Sobell, and Sobell, 1977; Keller, 1972(a), 1972(b)).

Correct or not, from a humane point of view the disease model is far superior to the heavy-handed moralizing and harsh social treatment previously lathered upon alcoholics in this society. But the emergence of the disease concept appears to have been more of a political and social triumph than a result of medical science and clinical research (much in the same way that the discovery of mental illness was by way of social reform rather than empirical research (Szasz, 1961)). For example, the discovery of alcoholism as a kind of allergic reaction to ethanol has, as near as can be determined, no basis in fact, no substantial empirical support. Rather, as Pattison (1976) recounts, it appears to have been a creation of the ample "folk-science medicine" of the 1930s, a product of the new blush of enthusiasm for the allergy theories of disease. One of the early friends of AA was a Dr. Silkworth, not coincidentally a prominent and influential New York internist and allergist (Pattison, 1976:414).

Critiques of the disease concept of alcoholism charge that it lacks anything but the most tentative clinical and research support; that it is a paradigm occasioned primarily by shifting political and social winds (not the least of which was the rising prominence of the medical profession in the 1930s); and that it continues to be influential because it is compatible with the current American tendency to "medicalize" moral, ethical, and social issues (Szasz, 1977). Disease concepts in general (especially the germ theory of disease of which the allergy paradigm is one variant) allow us, says Slater (1980), to see the organism as "invaded by dangerous aliens whose presence justifies military intervention by the healer" (p. 122). Thus, we want to "wipe out cancer," "fight" heart disease, deal muscular dystrophy a "knockout blow," etc. We fail to see within the metaphor of the "germ" that the organism is out of balance with its immediate ecological surroundings and internally warped (out of touch with body signals, tempos, and needs). One could well argue that most of the cancer and heart disease in this country is caused by our own profligate fouling of the environment—whether industrial pollution, food additives, or urban density (Slater, 1980). Individual and communal wholeness (the essence of health) loses out, always, to the prerogatives of the marketplace and the inane but energetic pursuit of materialism. Germ theory blinds us to this ecological reality.

We have the seeds of the social-psychological view. Stanton Peele (1975) puts it succinctly:

> ...an addiction exists when a person's attachment to a sensation, an object, or another person is such as to lessen his appreciation of and ability to deal with other things in the environment, or in himself, so that he has become increasingly dependent on that experience as his only source of gratification (p. 57).

In describing the signs of addiction, Slater (1981) paints a picture of an individual driven crazily and mistakenly to find in the addicting substance what it cannot possibly give: a sense of organismic wholeness, vitality, and a secure fund of personally relevant meaning. As the addiction becomes increasingly pervasive, the individual continues to narrow down the scope of life to the boundaries prescribed by the addicting object. Other natural desires and urges are dammed up as the addict futilely tries to extract life out of the bottle, syringe, or dollar bill. Fearing its insufficiency, the addict is consumed with increasing and protecting the supply of "stuff." And the addict is always (at least to a point) urged on in this monomania because the "jolt," the first swallow, the $1,000 bundle seem to promise to expand or control subjective experience (pp. 36-64).

The addict is driven to recapture or create anew a subjective experience, an experience satisfying and compelling because it seems to fill a void in consciousness, a missing piece of the self, a recession in the psychic economy. The nasty hook of this drivenness is that underneath the pattern of addiction, and the emergence of the self as "addict," is the corrosive suspicion that the addiction demonstrates, ipso facto, that the hole is there and can't be filled by the stuff. The widely advertised guilt of the "morning after" is, in part, a resentment and fear, seething and muted, that one has not got all of his or her psychic parts, that the hole in the psyche is swelling.

The other side of this coin is that whatever "wholeness" one might want to experience subjectively cannot be had without a degree of community, without an environment of support and challenge, dialectic and dialogue. In America, we still maintain the historically and culturally odd idea that the individual can do it alone, that autonomy is the apogee of human development, that perfect independence is possible. Yet, in a roundabout way, this delusion is fertilizer for the soil from which addiction sprouts (Slater, 1976).

2. *Addiction is not the exception, it is the rule.*

In our society now we are mightily concerned, in both a moral and medical sense, about addiction to substances that can be ingested, create alterations of consciousness, impair judgment, and occasionally lead to disastrous social consequences. These, though widespread and alarming in proportion, seem the exception. Of course, history shows us that, in some places and times, substances now regarded as dangerous were lauded for their magical, healthful, or socially and personally beneficient properties (Jaffe, 1979). The reverse is, naturally, true as well.

But the nature of human beings is that we can and do become addicted to anything: diet cola, money, sex, work, refined sugar, television, cards, etc. It is not particularly the substance, object, or experience that is addicting. Rather it is our need for symbolic resonance. Our capacity to elaborate symbolically allows us to attach importance, and idiosyncratic or collective meaning to inanimate and inert, or fully animate things. Even if we find, as we undoubtedly will—for an empirical certainty—that some substances do alter neurochemical functioning in such ways as to produce psychophysical "dependence," such dependence would require a prior symbolic commitment, a shift of orientation, an alteration of meaning. The studies of placebo vs. real drinking, and drinker expectancy, for example, suggest this (Marlatt, Demming & Reid, 1973; Pliner & Coppel, 1974). This very human phenomenon, called by Becker (1968:179) "fetishism," derives from the need to narrow down the scope of experience of the external world, to cut back out of fear, a sense of smallness, insignificance, and lack. The fetish object allows us to find meaning, conviction, ritual, and drama in a perilously small piece of the existential pie. It is the object of our addiction (and its presumed effects) that we fetishize. Be it alcohol, opiates, a person, or technological bric-a-brac (e.g., video games, home computers), we become addicted when we make a commitment to the objects as the source of personal meaning, when we give it existential authority. Naturally, the authority is rarely complete, but the addiction begins its course when the object *becomes fetish.*

Fetish objects vary enormously in the range of experience they allow, the degree of conviction they encourage, and the social and personal relevance of the meaning with which they are imbued. Societies characterized by lower rates of ingestion and addiction of alcohol, have already enhanced the object and the ritual or idiosyncratic act of ingestion with a kind of collective meaning that subordinates any given individual's meaning system ("This is a drink to be used to celebrate the passing of a season or a life transformation—nothing more, nothing less"). In our culture (and surely others), the erosion of communal meaning and collective support, the eruption of narcissism (Lasch, 1978), and the paradoxical and conflicting ideas we have about addictive substances (especially alcohol) make many of them attractive receptacles for distorted and shriveled existential meaning. Sadly, the more urgent and driven our fetishism, the more we cut ourselves off from other sources of meaning and the more we attempt to secure it from the petty and pathetic glass, syringe, or capsule.

All addictions are, existentially at any rate, blooms from the same bush. And since the problem of meaning is a central one for us all, the potential for addiction *is there* for us all. And if our culture thwarts meaning-making we find its caricature, fetishism, extraordinarily attractive and available. Were it not for this, the rickety ethics of the marketplace and the smarmy lures of the adman would soon pass to the cultural periphery.

An extension of these themes is that no substance or object is of itself addicting. The evidence on controlled drinking, the cultural variability in drinking rates and spontaneous remissions, for example, seem growing testimony to that (Pattison, 1976).

3. *A corollary to the above themes is that cultures and their social structures tend to exaggerate or depress the human propensity to addiction.*

It is known that alcohol addiction rates and the probabilities of becoming addicted vary between cultures (Reuband, 1977; Sulkunen, 1976) although reports tend to show that, in the Western world at least, alcohol consumption has generally been on the rise since World War II (Makela, 1978). Given the social psychological themes we have sounded thus far, we can hypothesize that there may be elements in American culture that excite the rate of addiction to all manner of substances.[1]

a) *The disappearance of community and the illusion of autonomy.* Given our limitations as organism—and our organismically critical requirements for sociability and dependence as we mature—to swathe the fragile self in the bunting of family, neighborhood, or community and, ensconced there, to find support, direction, meaning, and a system of symbols integrated in action is wholly natural. Yet, in American culture, we grow to act as if we needed no one else in the world (though the counterpoint to this may be something like our fascination with "romance" and the perverse and pervasive interest in the doings of "celebrities"). It is not, however, simply the illusion of the lonely self or even the falling away of community that is so critical here; it is the dichotomy between the two that culture forces upon us. And, says Roszak, "every dichotomy this culture clings to forces us to choose, and every choosing is a repressing, the exile of some outlawed part of ourselves" (Roszak, 1975: p. 154). Does the bottle seem to heal the rift? Does, for a moment, the effect of ethanol mimic the warmth and security of the repressed (but longed for) community without upstaging the preening ego? Perhaps.

b) *The prominence of "staple" - over "use" - values (Illich, 1977).* Staple values are those that either by implication or more directly support consumption, passivity, dependence, and an external locus of control. In a culture built of the raw materials of the marketplace, staple values have a peculiar logic. However, the orientation to the world, to the self, and to nature suggested by such values has led to a variety of delusions. Not the least of these is that we can *buy* human qualities (e.g., friendship or sexual allure); or solutions to human problems (e.g., a happy, exciting marriage); or states of mind (e.g., ecstacy). We turn away from our own internal resources, from the network of community and kinship knowledge, from the awareness rooted in the circumstances of everyday life, from trust in our own organism; and we turn to the sanctified countenance of the professional (or the affable charlatan posing as professional) at the technological bazaar. We become, then, less able to distinguish between felt needs and those needs (or wants) learned at the feet of culture, various advertisers, and assorted professionals (Illich, 1977: 28-29).

Use-values are created as we pursue interests and challenges directed and orchestrated by felt needs, as we grapple with problems emerging from the context of our daily life, and as we attempt to set the tempo, tone, and sense of everyday experience (attempting to create moments of satisfaction and pleasure, to make something, to ritualize important individual or collective transformations and the like).

Addiction is a statement about the supremacy of staple values. The addict is consumer par excellence, and in the act of buying, hoarding, and using, he or she has become immersed in and totally at the mercy of the marketplace. The dependence and passivity (vis-a-vis substance use, anyway) is the ultimate affirmation of staple values.[2] The addict is only doing, of course to himself, what many of us rely on the physician or professional to do—the chemical administration of mind, the stultification of the sense. We all can emerge as mindless consumers incapable of creating values from our own experience and encounters (Kovel, 1981). The inherent philosophy of commerce, business, and capital formation poises us all on the abyss of addiction.

c) *"Medical nemesis" (Illich, 1976).* Medicine has captured the field of alcoholism and addiction (to even call it a "field" presupposes a major concession to a single profession). This is not surprising considering the medicalization of many human trials and tribulations, quirks and flaws. Medicalization may or may not be justified in terms of clinical or laboratory discoveries about the nature of pathology. To surrender the understanding and control of a human condition in its variety to a profession or discipline is to foreclose certain ethical considerations, and to precipitously narrow the conception of that human activity. In addition, the power of the medical profession extends far beyond clinical boundaries as more and more human traits, lifestyles, and responses are considered "disease." "But psychiatrists should keep in mind that they are not truly medical; at most they are 'medico-social'. Since psychiatry has never been able to define mental disease, the medical basis for psychiatric authority must continue to be questioned, and psychiatric decisions that rely on medical authority must always be scrutinized"

(Robitscher, 1980:161).   In discussing the avid prescription of psychotropics, Halleck (1971) makes some points that might well apply to medicalization generally.   Medicalization presumes that the surrounding moral, social, and political topography of any human problem is merely background: there, but not important.   Medicalization amplifies the power of the physician, both in the immediate interpersonal sense of doctor/patient relationships and in the larger sense of sociopolitical influence.   (The current story of women, depression, and their treatment is, in no small way, a story of power inequalities, and social protest foreclosed by medicalization) (Tennov, 1975).   Finally, medicalization frequently leads to iatrogenic illness (pp. 71-77).

In a society where medicine and medical care and technology have become big business (consider medicine's links to the corporate pharmaceutical world) "...people come to believe that in health care, as in all other fields of endeavor, technology can be used to change the human condition according to almost any design" (Illich, 1976:73).   The addict, then, is only doing what officially we do as patients: passively consuming the magical elixirs that bathe our confused, dunned, or empty self with chemical balm.

d) *Group solidarity.*   David McClelland and others have developed a theory of alcohol use and abuse (with particular reference to males) based on cross-cultural research of the relationship between social solidarity and the need for personal power (McClelland et al., 1972).   Their research has been criticized for methodological flaws but, in fact, has been painstaking, replicative, and has employed sophisticated analytic techniques.   The central message of the research, as I see it, is this: In those societies where rates of heavy drinking and alcoholism are high, males are placed in a seemingly irresoluble predicament.   On the one hand, socialization is laced with an implicit and heavy demand to be assertive and interpersonally potent.   On the other, there is no reliable mechanism for providing and ritually transforming assertive behavior into permanent prestige and normative behavior.   The usual means for this consolidation in societies is ritual cohesion (and tradition) among groups of males.   These groups foster self-control and provide institutional means for the social integration of prestige and recognition. In the absence of these groups and in the face of the demand to be assertive, males often develop a clearly anarchic and high motivational need for personal power (nPower) called the "stud" cluster; an array of impulsive, dominating, aggressive kinds of behavior: drinking, exploitative sex, vicarious experience, prestige possession, manipulation of others.   This, of course, is not the only kind of power.   Effective power is *socialized* power, assertiveness in the service of ideals, or the social good, or the good of another individual.   In the research done so far, heavy drinkers and alcoholics (males) tend to be "studs" (Wanner, 1972:92-95; McClelland, 1972:164-66).   Our culture does demand from males an intense demand for self-assertion, but gives no communal context for that assertion to be transformed into prestige via the learning of self-control and sociability within a context of group solidarity.

    e. *"The Ego Mafia" (Slater, 1980)*. Americans, as we have noted before, are hopelessly and haplessly individualistic. We act *as if* we believe that, as Alan Watts once phrased it, "we are separate egos enclosed in a bag of skin" (Watts, 1966). We are dominated by our egos and the ego is a despot, refusing to let us hear from and respond to other constituent parts of the self—the body, fantasy, desires, moods, urges, and musings. And, in this hegemony of the ego, the henchmen are the Ego Mafia, that conspiratorial conclave of other egos having their way and bent on designing a world of straight lines, hierarchies, causes and effects—in other words, obsessive control (Slater, 1980:122).

    "The Ego Mafia exists, in large part, to de-emphasize our participation in the fabric of life. It likes to invent boundaries and pigeonholes—to classify and categorize and anlyze and find any way it can to break up (in our minds at least) this organic unit of living matter." (Slater, 1980:120). It lays the foundation of the basic fear that keeps it in business: we may never be quite good enough. If the Ego Mafia had not severed us from our natural knowledge and awareness of the whole self, we would not fall for its ruses; we would not be afraid. Thus "...the source of all addiction is the Ego's feeling that it is missing something and what it is missing is one of its own Constituents that it refuses to listen to" (Slater, 1980:121). The organization of our life around science, technology, bureaucratization, and the accumulation of wealth is a handiwork of the Ego Mafia. The cost to participate in this life is the lessening of the chance for fuller organismic experience.

    We are an addiction-prone society, then, driving people to seek a subjective jolt or soothing anesthetic because we have created institutions that increasingly narrow the range and depth of human experience and control, create the sense that something is missing or we are missing something, and then provide a variety of delightful and horrible but thoroughly sham ways to enliven personal experience or to mute panic. And those of us unfortunate enough to be entrapped in an addiction but seeking escape have only the hope that bureaucracy, pseudotechnology, and medicine can bring; pale hope considering that the assumptions that support them are often those which make addiction so necessary. In Kovel's (1980) words: "...social control...has become increasingly instrumental and invisible. No better way exists for capital[3] to meet these exigencies than to institute 'health ethics' in general, and of mental hygiene in particular, as the paramount criterion of what is socially desirable, bad, mad, or possessed: they are *sick*, and need the ministrations of a mental hygienist, the technically skilled, impersonal practitioner of a remunerable skill. And if they get too sick, they have to be put away, for their own good, or society's" (81-82). The point is not so much the obvious intervention but that *medical/bureaucratic enterprise extends the phenomenology of addiction* that we have been describing.

While a social psychological view of addiction and alcoholism is by no means complete or even necessarily logically coherent we can recount some of its elements. Addiction, broadly construed, is a common human phenomenon born of our capacity for symbolic construction of the self and driven by an organismic (total being) need for rootedness, stimulation, and a sense of wholeness. Symbolic constructs (like the self) are notoriously fragile and highly susceptible to the shaping hands of social forces of all kinds—interpersonal, institutional, cultural, and ideological. When the symbolic stuff out of which the self is made is insufficient, or full of contradictions or missing elements (think of the way we define men and women in our culture); and when our natural organismic striving is suppressed or diverted into narrow and inappropriate channels, it is not odd that addiction is one solution. And, in our culture, addiction succeeds for a variety of reasons. Not the least of these are that:

a) It is the one fetishistic alternative that extends or mimics the major cultural role we all play: consumer.

b) Addiction is encouraged. The marketplace would crumble were it not for the spectacular ability of the corporate commercial world to induce appetite and insatiability in us (Kovel, 1981). But for addicts the object of appetite must perform a deeper transformative act: a reconstruction, filling out, or numbing of the self.

c) Finally, the disease model of addiction and alcoholism may not be appropriate, not just because of the lack of evidence, but because the medical approach to understanding and intervening exacerbates some of the very phenomena that may be a part of the insistent human capacity for addiction—separation, disunity, and technologizing (fetishizing).

Stanton Peele (1976) distinguishes the addict from the nonaddict simply and well:

"The ability to derive a positive pleasure from something, to do something because it brings joy to oneself, is, in fact, a principal criterion of nonaddiction. It might seem a foregone conclusion that people take drugs for enjoyment, yet this is not true of addicts. An addict does not find heroin pleasurable in itself. Rather, he uses it to obliterate other aspects of the environment [and himself, I might add] that he dreads" (63).

Disharmonies
1. *The problem of the body..*

Our social psychological perspective, while calling for a full organismic view of things, ignores, in essence, the biology of addiction. The research attempting to sort this out has not produced much of a substantial nature, although the leads with respect to the connection of bipolar depression and alcoholism (Taylor and Abrams, 1981) with some of the newer work on the biosociology of "craving" (Milkman and Sunderwirth, 1983; Erikson and Ewen, 1983) are suggestive. The fact remains, however, that no theory of addiction will go very far without dealing with the biological substrate of addiction (as either etiological or as sequelae).

2.   *The phenomenological problem.*
      The subtleties of clinical and empirical debate aside, our everyday encounters with the addicted do suggest—"verstehen"—a difference between the alcoholic and nonalcoholic. Many addicts do appear to be insanely driven, rapidly decompensating, and careening into social disrepute and physiological disrepair. The prevailing social imagery of the alcoholic (as in *The Lost Weekend* and *The Days of Wine and Roses*) is convincing. But we must remain circumspect. Our subjective and symbolic fashions may come from inner or cultural motives, or they may be based on a highly select and skewed sample of experiences. Nevertheless, it *is* difficult to reconcile everyday constructions with the more esoteric productions of the theorist.

3.   *The trivialization problem.*
      To propose different orientations to social problems runs the risk of making inane or trivial what for thousands of individuals and families has been tragic. Weiner says it pointedly: "...inherent in such sociological and psychological theorizing is the danger of imparting the feeling that there really is no problem. Thus, while such theories have had a notable impact on changing perspectives on *just what constitutes* the problem, an equally sizeable impact has been the manner in which such theorizing has divided some people within the recovery-service and volunteer-action worlds from their counterparts within the research world" (102). No theory should ever subvert the attempt to understand, in detail and as clearly as possible, *what it is like to be addicted to something.*

4.   *The treatment problem.*
      The medical model seems more clearly tied, for obvious reasons, to treatment, control, and prevention policy and method. This is not so evident in the social psychological realm. However, and for whatever reasons, the medical model has not yet prevented the problem of addiction from extending itself like an insatiable amoeba. From a social psychological perspective, Slater (1980) offers some general, orienting suggestions. We must create institutions that discourage addiction. We must create institutions that support other motivations. And we must increase popular consciousness about the miseries of addiction and the joys that appear when we discard it (156). Thus, short of a major institutional or cultural upheaval, the social psychological view suggests that some individual

addicts will continue to be helped, by whatever means, but the problem of addiction will continue to seep into the backwaters and reservoirs of cultural and social life until we are able to reunite mind and body, self and community, meaning and ritual in the deepest marrow of culture and social institution.

In the final analysis, the current debate over whether alcoholics can be cured and choose to drink normally or are forever flawed with an incurable illness boils down to a question about the nature of the self. The social psychological portrait of the self suggests that the self can be converted and transformed and reach fuller organismic experience, thus making fetishization a poverty-stricken choice for life. To make the point and to stake out the difference between the social psychological view and the medical model, William Barrett's recounting of the experience of the renowned writer, Dashiell Hammett, will serve:

> Hammett, a heavy drinker for years, had reached the advanced stage of alcoholism accompanied by delirium tremens. His doctor told him that he would be dead in a month if he continued drinking. Hammett said he would go on the wagon; but the doctor told Lillian Hellman, Hammet''s good friend, "He can't and he won't." But Hammett did go on the wagon and stayed there. Five or six years later, when Miss Hellman told him what the doctor had said to her, Hammett looked puzzled and observed, "But I gave the man my word, then, that day." (Barrett, 1979:303)

It was the meaning provided by a brash, symbolically reconstitutive assertion that allowed Hammett to thwart his alien passion, booze.

NOTES

1. It is not clear whether the U.S.A. has a very high risk culture for addiction (to alcohol or anything else), but it does appear that in terms of the level of consumption per capita of wine, beer, and spirits we are toward the upper third of countries for which data is available—and moving up. (Sulkunen, 1976)

2. Joel Kovel (1981) reminds us that capitalism drives a wedge between us as members of a political economy (essentially consumers) and as human beings with the capacity for desire (sensing, feeling, understanding, expressing); it fills us with the notion that we can purchase desire (its trivial and fake substitutes, really) on the marketplace. The addict is, in this case, perhaps the most duped among us.

3. And, no doubt, the topheavy, oppressive bureaucracies of totalitarian societies—again, the craft of the Ego Mafia.

REFERENCES

Barrett, W.
1979 The Illusion of Technique. New York: Anchor Press Doubleday.
Becker, E.
1968 The Structure of Evil. New York: George Braziller.
Erickson, C. K., and W. L. Ewen
1983 The Clinical Promise of Naturally-Occurring Addictive Substances in Alcohol Addiction. The Magazine of the Texas Commission on Alcoholism 9:19–20.
Halleck, S. L.
1971 The Politics of Therapy. New York: Science House.
Illich, I. D.
1976 Medical Nemesis: The Expropriation of Health. New York: Pantheon.
Illich, I. D.
1977 Disabling Professions. Salem, N.H.: M. Boyars.
Jaffe, J. H.
1979 "Addictive Disorders—An Interface Between Medicine and Politics." In Addiction Research and Treatment: Converging Trends, edited by E. L. Gottheil, A. T. McClellan, K. A. Druley, and A. I. Alterman. New York: Pergamon Press.
Jellinek, E. M.
1946 Phases in the Drinking History of Alcoholics. Quarterly Journal of Studies on Alcohol 7:1–88.
Jellinek, E. M.
1960 The Disease Concept of Alcoholism. New Brunswick, N.J.: Hillhouse Press.
Keller, M.
1972(a) On the Loss-of-Control Phenomenon in Alcoholism. The British Journal of The Addictions 67:153–166.
Keller, M.
1972(b) The Oddities of Alcoholics. Quarterly Journal of Studies on Alcohol 33:1147–1148.
Kovel, J.
1980 "The American Mental Health Industry." In Critical Psychiatry: The Politics of Mental Health, edited by D. Ingleby. New York: Pantheon Books.
Kovel, J.
1981 The Age of Desire. New York: Pantheon Books.
Lasch, C.
1978 The Culture of Narcissism. New York: Norton.

McClelland, D. C., E. Wanner, and R. Vanneman
1972 "Drinking in the Wider Context of Restrained and Unrestrained Assertive Thoughts and Acts." In *The Drinking Man*, edited by D. C. McClelland, W. N. David., R. Kalin, and E. Wanner. New York: The Free Press.
Makela, K.
1978 "Level of Consumption and Social Consequences of Drinking." In *Research Advances in Alcohol and Drug Problems*, edited by Y. Israel, F. B. Glaser, H. Kalant, R. E. Popham, W. Schmidt, and R. G. Smart. Vol. 4. New York: Plenum Press.
Marlatt, G. A., B. Demming, and J. B. Reid
1973 Loss of Control Drinking in Alcoholics: An Experimental Analogue. *Journal of Abnormal Psychology* 81:233–241.
Milkman, H., and S. Sunderwirth
1983 The Chemistry of Craving. *Psychology Today* 17(Oct.):36–44.
Pattison, E. M.
1976 "Nonabstinent Drinking Goals in the Treatment of Alcoholics."   In *Research Advances in Alcohol and Drug Problems*, edited by R. J. Gibbins, Y. Israel, H. Kalant, R. E. Popham, W. Schmidt and R. G. Smart. Vol. 3. New York: John Wiley and Sons.
Pattison, E. M., M. N. Sobell, and L. C. Sobell
1977 *Emerging Concepts of Alcohol Dependence*. New York: Springer.
Peele, S., with A. Brodsky
1975 *Love and Addiction*. New York: New American Library.
Pliner, P., and H. Cappell
1974 Modification of Affective Consequences of Alcohol: A Comparison of Social and Solitary Drinking. *Journal of Abnormal Psychology* 83:418–425.
Reuband, K. H.
1977 "The Pathological and Subcultural Model of Drug Use—A Test of Two Contrasting Explanations." In *Alcoholism and Drug Dependence: A Multidisciplinary Approach*, edited by J. S. Madden, R. Walker and W. H. Kenyon. New York: Plenum Press.
Robitscher, J.
1980 *The Powers of Psychiatry*. Boston: Houghton-Mifflin.
Roszak, T.
1975 *Unfinished Animal: The Aquarian Frontier and the Evolution of Consciousness*. New York: Harper/Colophon.
Slater, P.
1976 *The Pursuit of Loneliness*. Boston: Beacon Press.
Slater, P.
1980 *Wealth Addiction*. New York: E. P. Dutton.
Sulkunen, P.
1976 "Drinking Patterns and the Level of Alcohol Consumption: An International Overview." In *Research Advances in Alcohol and Drug Problems*, edited by R. J. Gibbins, Y. Israel, H. Kalant, R. E. Popham, W. Schmidt, and R. G. Smart. Vol. 3. New York: John Wiley and Sons.

Szasz, T. S.
1961   *The Myth of Mental Illness: Foundations of a Theory of Personal Conduct.*
New York: Harper and Row (Hoeber Medical Division).
Szasz, T. S.
1977   *The Theology of Medicine: The Political-Philosophical Foundations of Medical Ethics.* Baton Rouge: Louisiana State University Press.
Taylor, M. A., and R. Abrams
1981   Early- and Late-Onset Bipolar Illness.   *Archives of General Psychiatry* 38:58–61.
Tennov. D.
1976   *Psychotherapy: The Hazardous Cure.* New York: Anchor Press/ Doubleday.
Wanner, E.
1972   "Power and Inhibition: A Revision of the Magical Potency Theory." In *The Drinking Man*, edited by D. C. McClelland, W. N. Davis, R. Kalin, and E. Wanner. New York: The Free Press.
Weiner, C. L.
1981   *The Politics of Alcoholism: Building an Arena Around a Social Problem.* New Brunswick, N.J.: Transaction Books.
Watts, A.
1966   *The Book: On the Taboo Against Knowing Who You Are.* New York: Collier Books.

THE MEDICALIZATION OF ALCOHOLISM: DISCONTINUITIES IN IDEOLOGIES OF DEVIANCE
Robert E. Tournier

Over the last few decades, there has been a progressive abandonment of a moral-deviance conception of alcoholism and an acceptance of a more modern disease concept. In some respects this can be argued to be, in part, illusion, with the disease concept only shallowly covering older, less potentially therapeutic perspectives. The purposes of this paper, data for which are derived from research conducted on attitudes of alcohol and drug program professionals, are twofold: first, to briefly examine the sociohistorical origins of the disease concept of alcoholism and of its ready acceptance, at least among professionals; second, to explore the degree to which the disease concept has been accepted by those professionals, not simply on the level of affirmation, but on the level of an acceptance of its implications.

The history of both public and professional conceptions of alcoholism has been marked by a pervasive historiographic myopia. Popular sentiment regards the pre–twentieth century as an age of medical superstition and of a readiness to regard the alcoholic as immoral, irresponsible, damned, or weak. While such attitudes certainly existed, and still clearly do, it is important to recall that as early as the last days of the eighteenth century, there was an apparent willingness on behalf of at least a minority of "experts" to define alcoholism as an illness rather than as a moral failing, and the alcoholic as victim rather than sinner.

Benjamin Rush's 1785 *Inquiry into the Effects of Ardent Spirits Upon the Human Body and Mind*—predictably dismissed by Szasz (1970:140) as psychiatric imperialism through which "Rush was composing propaganda against alcohol, making full use of the rhetoric of medicine"—set the stage for a nineteenth-century redefinition of the problem. Trotter's 1804 *An Essay, Mental, Philosophical, and Chemical on Drunkenness* and Kain's 1828 "On Intemperance Considered as a Disease" opened the century; in 1866 the French physician Gabriel first used the term *alcoholism* in its modern sense; *the Journal of Inebriety*, founded in 1876, championed an "alcoholism as illness" perspective, and from its founding until it ceased publication in 1913, published more than eighty papers and editorials on a disease concept of alcoholism (Keller, 1976).

Robert E. Tournier received his Ph.D. in sociology from Tulane University in 1972. He is currently an associate professor in the Department of Sociology at The College of Charleston in Charleston, South Carolina. His current research interests in alcohol and drug abuse include the evolution and internal consistency of perceptions of addictions, as well as the kinds of helper-helped relationships that are presumed to result in staff burnout.

One of the vagaries of the historiography of ideologies of alcoholism is a basic disagreement over the relevance of these nineteeth-century views to twentieth-century thought. Keller (1976), the best known and one of the most influential advocates of a disease concept, sees the modern "alcoholism as illness" ideology as a logical and inevitable extension of a way of viewing the problem which dates from as early as the first century. MacAndrew (1969:492), on the other hand, an outspoken critic of the disease concept, dismisses the eighteenth- and nineteenth-century writers as unimportant and *The Journal of Inebriety* as the "organ of a very small minority within the American medical profession" which, when it finally ceased publication, "was greeted less with sorrow or jubilation than with a yawn."

Whether important or not, such "modern" ideologies disappeared by the mid-nineteenth century, as a flood of temperance propaganda broke across the land (see, for example, Rorabaugh, 1979), and as temperance movement-based values came to dominate our view of alcoholics and their problems. It is against this background, I believe, that the so-called Alcoholism Movement and its rediscovery of the disease concept must be viewed.

In what is probably the most influential book written on the nature of alcoholism in the twentieth century, *Disease Concept of Alcoholism* (1960), E. M. Jellinek revived as a working hypothesis the idea that alcoholism is a disease state: the alcoholic is neither weak nor morally depraved but is ill and should be treated accordingly. Much of the appeal of Jellinek's work lay in the fact that the climate was clearly ready for a rejection of the old "drunkenness" stereotypes: in 1946, the General Assembly of the Presbyterian Church accepted a motion that alcoholism was a disease (Roueche, 1960); in 1956, the Board of the American Medical Association passed a resolution urging hospitals to admit alcoholics on the basis of clinical indications alone (American Medical Association, 1968), a resolution seconded in 1957 by the American Hospital Association.   Jellinek's work thus found a ready audience and was to have an enormous impact on contemporary conceptions of alcoholism.

Much of the readiness with which Jellinek's "alcoholism as disease" hypothesis was accepted is a result of its adoption, by a wide variety of interests, as an intellectual foundation for positions already held.   For members of Alcoholics Anonymous, Jellinek's work was seized upon not only because of his early connection with the movement in the development of both his "natural history" approach to alcoholism and his taxonomic conception of the diversity of alcohol-related problems (Leach and Norris, 1977), but also because of the ease with which the disease concept would be interpreted (and misinterpreted) in support of a rather naive allergy theory of alcoholism which is somewhat parallel to, but not at all identical with, what Jellinek was proposing (Patterson, Sobell and Sobell, 1977; Keller, 1972).

For the National Council on Alcoholism—perhaps the foremost lobby for the alcoholic in our society—Jellinek's ideas were adopted as the cornerstone to what was to become a massive and enduring public relations campaign which had as its goal the destigmatization of alcoholism and of the alcoholic.

For professionals, and for the more frequently found paraprofessionals in the substance abuse field—many of whom were recovered substance abusers themselves—the Jellinek-inspired disease concept of alcoholism was enthusiastically accepted and very quickly became a part of their vocabulary of motives.

There are a great many reasons for the rapid spread of Jellinek's ideas. Part of the attraction was indisputably humanitarian and derived from a general rejection of the nineteenth-century stigmatization of alcoholics as inappropriate and, more important, as counterproductive. Particularly with the popularization of the concept of "loss of control" as the dynamic factor in the continuation of dysfunctional drinking, it became possible to conceptualize substance abusers as neither depraved nor willfully deviant, but as sick and inexorably trapped in a situation from which they are unable to escape without help.

Another part of the attraction derived from a recognition of the important part that a medical/disease model might play in treatment and in eventual recovery. The benefits are indisputable. In the first place, to the degree to which excessive drinkers in our society are stigmatized and subject to overt social rejection, their problems are aggravated and their potential for recovery lessened. If an "alcoholism as illness" label can be successfully applied and accepted by both alcoholics and those responsible for their care, this tendency toward stigmatization and consequent rejection—while not precluded—can be significantly reduced.

In the second place, it is far easier to mobilize social support for treatment than for punishment. While it is not necessary that we agree with Platt (1967:33) that it is a "belief in our culture...that treatment to prevent...suffering and to restore physical and social functioning should be provided," it is nonetheless probable that an appeal for treatment will be significantly more productive than a defense of the attitude of "therapeutic nihilism" that characterized an earlier age.

Finally, there is at least some indication that, to the degree to which alcoholics can be encouraged to accept the sickness label with all that it implies, they will not as readily adopt the complex set of denial/projection/rationalization mechanisms that represent such a difficult impediment to treatment and will be motivated to play a more active role in their own recovery.

There is yet another aspect to this, one which is latent but in many respects equal in importance to those already discussed. The disease model has the effect of establishing alcohol-related problems as clearly medical in nature, and by doing so, fixes "responsibility for...care of the alcoholic...upon the physician and his paramedical partners" (Gitlow, 1973:7). While this is of no particular importance to physicians, many of whom seem to dislike dealing with alcoholics anyway, it is of enormous importance to the marginal professionals and paraprofessionals who serve as the rank and file of treatment programs, for it allows them to identify with a medical model and to assume what is essentially a medical role.

It would, of course, be a mistake to conclude that an "alcoholism as illness" prespective is universally affirmed. There is a small but extremely vocal minority which, in their rejection of the traditional AA based ideas of "loss of control" (see, especially, Patterson, Sobell and Sobell, 1977) and their espousal of controlled drinking as an appropriate treatment goal for behaviorally oriented therapy, advocate a view of alcoholism as learned behavior. Nevertheless, it is important to recognize that the medical model not only remains the standard against which other ideologies are inevitably measured, but is also the one most aggressively popularized both to professionals and to the general public.

The Problem

In spite of almost a generation of advocacy, there is substantial evidence that full acceptance of the "alcoholism as illness" dictum has not yet been realized. Mulford and Miller reported, for example, in their 1964 study, that only some 24 percent of a public sample gave unqualified endorsement to a disease concept of alcoholism, while 41 percent endorsed a rather ambivalent combination of medical and moralistic points of view.

In a later study undertaken on a sample of undergraduate college students, Orcutt (1976) found a quite similar pattern: some 36 percent endorsed a strictly disease concept of alcoholism, and 54 percent endorsed a combined medical/moral point of view. Orcutt, on the basis of these findings, concluded that a mixed, moralistic-medical ideology was currently the most important point of view, at least among college students.

In a still later study, Orcutt, Cairl, and Miller (1980) sought to extend their analysis beyond college students to explore, among other things, the fashion in which ideologies of alcoholism varied across different social control and service delivery organizations. In general, their findings revealed a rather strong, moral-medical bias among a sample of police officers, and a rather strong medical orientation among a sample of workers from an alcohol/drug detoxification facility. They concluded that "on a continuum from the law enforcement sample to the detoxification sample, with the public sample in the middle,...we find a clear pattern of increasing acceptance of the strongly 'medical' image of deviance" (pp. 656).

The present study is an extension of earlier work on ideologies of alcoholism to the specific beliefs held by alcohol and drug program personnel. While Orcutt, Cairl, and Miller (1980) dealt with a small and highly specialized portion of this population—specifically with staff members of a detoxification facility—we should be, I believe, very reluctant to generalize from individuals whose major concern is with the specifically medical aspects of alcoholism to all alcoholism program workers.

There is, without a doubt, a significant affirmation of a medical model of alcoholism among those who deal with alcoholics. This, of course, follows from the nature of their professional and occupational socialization as well as from what might be presumed to be an interest in the kind of dignification of one's work and of one's client which accompanies a medical ideology. The kind of medical ideology which they hold is, however, a matter of empirical concern, for if it is but a superficially held veneer, such a situation would have serious consequences for program functioning.

Methodology

Data for this study were derived from questionnaires administered to participants in a week long, state-level alcohol and drug school as part of a broader study of the impact of short-term training experiences on attitudes toward substance abuse and substance abusers. Usable study N was 157, although totals vary slightly from table to table as not all respondents answered all questions.

Subjects in the study represent a broad spectrum of positions and responsibilities vis-a-vis alcohol/alcoholism. Almost half (48 percent) were directly employed by alcohol/drug agencies, most commonly in counseling positions (53 percent). The next largest block of subjects were education/ prevention personnel (23 percent), most of whom were actively engaged in education/prevention-related activities. As a group, the subjects were relatively young (61 percent were thirty-four or younger), generally inexperienced (62 percent had been employed in drug/alcohol-related jobs for two years or less), and rather highly educated (89 percent had had at least some college and 54 percent had had at least some graduate education). Lacking, as we do, a general picture of the staff composition of drug/alcohol-related programs, it is impossible to make any valid statements pertaining to generalizability.

Embedded in the opening session questionnaire for the school were four of the items used in the Orcutt, Cairl, and Miller (1980) study, responses to which were Likert in form:

"Alcoholics tend to be weak-willed people."
"An alcoholic should be viewed and treated as a person who is ill."
"A person should not be held responsible for being an alcoholic."
"I would feel uncomfortable if I had to be around alcoholics a lot."

The first and second items were used to construct a typology of ideologies of alcoholism, the categories of which form the basis for the analysis of data.

Table I. Ideologies of Alcoholism*

Response to Morality Item (Weak-Willed)	Response to Medical Item (Ill)	Derived Ideology
Agree	Agree	Moral-sickness
Agree	Disagree	Moralistic
Disagree	Agree	Medical
Disagree	Disagree	Behavioristic**

*   Adopted from Orcutt, Cairl, and Miller (1980).
** The behavioristic ideology is a residual category. Those who reject both the morality item and the medical item are presumed to affirm an essentially behavioristic ideology.

RESULTS
Professional Ideologies of Alcoholism
    The critical question with which one must deal when examining professional ideologies of alcoholism is the degree to which the disease concept has taken root among those whose work brings them into regular contact with alcoholics. My data, within which the detoxification component is virtually irrelevant (only 3 percent of the sample), paints a picture of ideologies of alcoholism which is, in some respects, quite different from that described by Orcutt, Cairl, and Miller (1980), and which suggests that alcoholism professionals, as a group, occupy an ideological position which, in terms of an affirmation of a medical model of alcoholism, lies between the Orcutt, et al. "public" sample on the one hand, and the detoxification facility sample on the other—a position characterized by a less than universal affirmation of the disease concept.
    What has occurred in the Orcutt work, I believe, is that the use of a sample of detoxification facility staff as representative of the sorts of ideologies characteristic of drug and alcohol professionals has led to an exaggeration of the proportion committed to a strictly medical model. This has generated a picture of professional ideologies of alcoholism which is rather more optimistic than is appropriate.

Table II: Comparison of Ideologies of Alcoholism

Ideology	Orcutt "Public" N=200	D and A School N=157	Orcutt "Detox" N=35
Moral-Sickness	59%	30%	29%
Moralistic	5%	5%	3%
Medical	34%	50%	66%
Behavioristic	2%	16%	3%

Chi-square=52.96 6 d.f.; p=.001

Internal Consistency

One of the major sources of attractiveness of a medical/disease model of alcoholism is a recognition of its utility in the destigmatization of the substance abuser. There are at least two aspects to this. In the first place, to the extent to which the alcoholics are ill, their actions are not a matter of volition but are rather the result of the operation of a disease state. Alcoholics can then be thought of as having no more control over alcohol consumption than the diabetic has over sugar metabolization. In the second place, to the extent to which alcoholics are ill, they are neither intrinsically dangerous nor threatening (as the disease is not communicable), but are deserving of sympathy and assistance. One could presume, then, that to the degree to which a disease concept has fully taken root there would be neither a significant attribution of responsibility nor any appreciable stigmatization. While it would be naive to presume that either would be entirely absent, one could hypothesize that they would be far less for those characterized by medical or behavioristic ideologies than for those whose ideologies contain morality components.

Perhaps the most striking element vis-a-vis the internal consistency of ideologies of alcoholism is a clear absence of consistency in the attitudes of many of those bearing medical and behavioristic ideologies.

Social Thought on Alcoholism

Table III. Responsibility by Ideology of Alcoholism

Attribution of Responsibility	Ideology of Alcoholism Moral/Moral-Sickness	Med./Behavioristic
Responsible	85% (51)	81% (78)
Not responsible	15% (9)	19% (18)

Gamma=.133 Chi-square=.360 2 d.f.; p=n.s.

One can reasonably presume a tendency towards an attribution of responsibility to the alcoholic by those whose attitudes are characterized by a morality component. This is indeed what our data demonstrate. On the other hand, to the degree to which a medical or behavioristic ideology defines the alcoholic as victim, one would expect that a significant proportion of bearers of such ideologies would not hold them responsible for their plight. This is clearly not the case, for of the ninety-six subjects who affirmed either a medical or a behavioristic ideology, 81 percent felt that a person should be held responsible for being an alcoholic.

The data pertaining to stigmatization are no less inconsistent.

Table IV: Stigmatization by Ideology of Alcoholism

Stigmatization	Ideology of Alcoholism Moral/Moral-Sickness	Med./Behavioristic
Comfortable	71% (39)	72% (73)
Uncomfortable	29% (16)	28% (28)

Gamma=-.034 Chi-square=.033 2 d.f.; p=n.s.

On an aggregate basis, 72 percent of our subjects indicated that they felt, or believed that they would feel, comfortable around alcoholics. But the distribution of responses (virtually identical for the medical/behavioral and the morality/moral-sickness ideologies) suggests that while the level of stigmatization is, overall, quite low, acceptance of a medical or behavioral ideology does little to further reduce it.

Drug and Alcohol Helping Personnel and Client Stereotypes

We have seen the fashion in which medical and behavioral ideologies of deviance show a tendency toward internal inconsistency and toward a persistence of stigmatization manifested in reported feelings of discomfort. It might be argued that many of those in our sample have either no regular contact with alcoholics (educators) or the kinds of contacts that take place only with the most disreputable alcoholics in our society (law enforcement personnel), and there is, therefore, no "reality" against which to test stereotypes. What of those who work directly with alcoholics? Is it not possible that their experiences serve as a panacea to the sort of persistence of stereotypes which characterize others?

Table V: Responsibility by Contact

Attribution of Responsibility	Contact	
	High Contact	Low Contact
Responsible	81% (76)	70% (44)
Not responsible	19% (18)	30% (19)

Gamma=.292 Chi-square=2.305 2 d.f.; p=n.s.

An examination of attribution of responsibility broken down by employment (High contact: alcohol/drug program personnel and social service workers. Low contact: law enforcement and education/prevention workers) lends very little support to what one might expect, for those whose work brings them into regular contact with alcoholics have somewhat higher expectations of client responsibility than those who have less regular contact. While the difference is neither large nor particularly significant, it still runs contrary to what one might reasonably expect. What of stigmatization?

Social Thought on Alcoholism

Table VI: Stigmatization by Contact

Stigmatization	Contact	
	High Contact	Low Contact
Comfortable	80% (67)	58% (37)
Uncomfortable	20% (17)	42% (27)

Gamma=.484 Chi-square=8.370 2 d.f.; p=.01

It is only in the realm of stigmatization that one's expectations are borne out, for those whose jobs bring them into regular contact with alcoholics are somewhat less likely to feel uncomfortable around alcoholics than are those who have little contact with them.

Discussion

In the *First Special Report to Congress*, the National Institute on Alcohol and Alcoholism (Secretary of Health, Education and Welfare, 1971:85) reported with some pride that "the legal status of...alcoholics in this country has changed dramatically in the short space of only 5 years," and that in the years since 1966, more progress had been made toward the medical handling of alcoholism, at least in the courts, than had been made in the three and a half centuries since the passage of the first public intoxication law in England in 1606. Perhaps, but our data lead to a somewhat different conclusion, for they suggest that the kinds of changes which characterize the judicial realm are not necessarily accompanied by parallel changes in conceptions of the alcoholic and of their problems, at least among some of those responsible for their care.

After several decades of strenuous advocation of a disease concept of alcoholism, those who work with and around alcoholics quite readily affirm an essentially "alcoholism as illness" position: in our data as well as in that of Orcutt (1977; 1980), the overwhelming majority of all subjects expressed agreement with the statement "An alcoholic should be viewed and treated as a person who is ill" (see Table II). And yet, in spite of this apparently clear medical orientation, there is also an equally clear ambivalence, for a significant proportion also endorse a position with a distinct moral bias.

Further analysis of the data suggest that the situation is more complex than suggested by the paradigm with which Orcutt, Cairl, and Miller (1980) operate (Table I). Not only do a large proportion of respondents who agree with an "alcoholism as illness" statement also agree with an "alcoholism as weakness" statement; more important, among those who affirm a strict medical ideology by explicitly rejecting the morality/weakness item, there is a clear tendency toward both internal inconsistency in their ideology and a persistence of a tendency toward stigmatization not suggested by Orcutt's paradigm; some 83 percent of the sample believe that alcoholics are responsible for their situation (Table III), a view at least partially at variance with the intent and implications of the disease concept of alcoholism; some 28 percent of the sample appear to respond to alcoholics in terms of some of the old stereotypes, for they report an expectation of discomfort at being around them (Table IV).

What conclusions can be drawn? In the first place, our data suggest that in spite of several decades of aggressive advocation, the disease concept of alcoholism has not fully taken root except as what may be a rather thin veneer over what are still apparently deeply rooted stereotypes. Granted, eight out of ten respondents agree with an "alcoholism as illness" statement, but our data suggest that this may be simply a mechanical obeisance to a position perceived as "proper." Tables V and VI suggest, furthermore, that at least in our sample, most alcohol and drug program workers still believe that alcoholics are in some fashion responsible for their plight and (inferentially) can somehow will themselves to recovery.

In the second place, our data suggest that Orcutt's belief that the medical-weakness ideology is a transition between the "old" moral-weakness prejudice and the "new" medical ideology may be premature, for only a small proportion of our drug and alcohol program workers hold a wholly consistent medical position.

Finally, our data suggest what may be a fundamental flaw in treatment/service delivery efforts. There seems always to have been some concern about the relative intractability of alcoholism, for once the problem reaches the point where functional impairment necessitates intervention, recoveries are won only with the most determined effort, and multiple relapses are extremely common. Certainly, with selected clients—particularly those with early stage, nonaddictive alcoholism who are still employed and who have been able to maintain both community respectability and viable interpersonal ties—the prognosis is extremely favorable, and success rates in the 70 to 80 percent range are quite possible. For a general population of alcoholics, however, particularly addictive alcoholics, success rates are discouragingly low, and at least some suspect that such recoveries as do occur take place for reasons quite unrelated to our best treatment efforts (see, for example, Storm and Cutter, 1969).

We have traditionally sought to explain the alcoholic's poor prognosis by reference to the concept of loss of control, as well as to the insidious nature of the disease and its impact on the alcoholic's life circumstances. Our data suggest another possibility: that programs designed to be therapeutic and to deliver services to alcoholics based upon an "officially" expressed medical model may be, in their implementation, at least partially punitive because of the attitudes and expectations of many of those with whom the alcoholic comes into contact. To the degree to which the alcoholic is held to be responsible for his/her plight, any therapeutic advantage which might occur from perceiving him/her as victim is lost, and potentially inappropriate expectations are made. The stage is set for a self-fulfilling prophecy, for, to the degree to which there is an attribution of responsibility, the inevitable relapses which accompany recovery are interpretable as willful irresponsibility and may well be reacted to accordingly. The result: lack of support, lack of reassurance, further psychological elaboration. It is this with which we must be concerned, for while the potentially therapeutic implications of a medical model are indisputable, to ignore counselor attitude and counselor-client interaction is to ignore what may well be its most important component.

REFERENCES

American Medical Association
  1968   *Manual of Alcoholism.* Chicago: American Medical Association.
Gitlow, S. E
  1973   "Alcoholism: A Disease." In *Alcoholism: Progress in Research and Treatment,* edited by P. Bourne and R. Fox. New York: Academic Press.
Jellinek, E. M.
  1960   *The Disease Concept of Alcoholism.* Highland Park, Ill.: Hillhouse Press.
Keller, M.
  1972   The Oddities of Alcoholics.   *Quarterly Journal of Studies on Alcohol.* XXX:1147-8.
Keller, M.
  1976   The Disease Concept of Alcoholism Revisited.   *Journal of Studies on Alcohol.* XXXVII:1694-1717.
Leach, B., and J. L. Norris
  1977   "Factors in the Development of Alcoholics Anonymous." In *The Biology of Alcoholism,* edited by B. Kisson and H. Begleiter. Vol. V: *Treatment and Rehabilitation of the Chronic Alcoholic.* New York: Plenum.
MacAndrew, C.
  1969   "On the Notion That Certain Persons Who Are Given to Frequent Drunkenness Suffer From a Disease Called Alcoholism." In *Changing Perspective in Mental Illness,* edited by S. C. Plog and R. B. Edgerton. New York: Holt, Rinehart and Winston.
Mulford, H. A., and D. E. Miller
  1964   Measuring Public Acceptance of the Alcoholic as a Sick Person. *Quarterly Journal of Studies on Alcohol* XXV:314-23.
Orcutt, J. D.
  1976   Ideological Variations in the Structure of Deviant Types.   *Social Forces* LV:419-37.

Orcutt, J. D., R. E. Cairl, and E. T. Miller
1980   Professional and Public Conceptions of Alcoholism. *Journal of Studies on Alcohol* XLI:652-61.
Patterson, E. M.
1973   "The Differential Utilization of Manpower." In *The Paraprofessional in the Treatment of Alcoholism: A New Profession*, edited by G. E. Staub and L. Kent. Springfield, Ill.: Charles C. Thomas.
Patterson, E. M., M. B. Sobell, and L. C. Sobell
1977   *Emerging Concepts of Alcohol Dependence*. New York: Springer.
Plaut, T. F.
1967   *Alcohol Problems: A Report to the Nation*. New York: Oxford University Press.
Rorabaugh, W. J.
1979   *The Alcoholic Republic: An American Tradition*. New York: Oxford University Press.
Roueche, B.
1960   *The Neutral Spirit: A Portrait of Alcohol*. Boston: Little, Brown and Company.
Secretary of Health, Education, and Welfare
1971   *First Special Report to the U.S. Congress on Alcohol and Health*. Washington, D.C.: U.S. Government Printing Office.
Storm, T., and R. E. Cutter
1969   "Treated and Untreated Alcoholics: Some Reflections on the Role of Treatment in the Process of Recovery from Alcoholism." In *Selected Papers*, North American Association of Alcoholism Programs. Washington, D.C.: North American Association of Alcoholism Programs.
Szasz, T. S.
1970   *The Manufacture of Madness*. New York: Dell Publishing Co.

SIN OR SOLACE? RELIGIOUS VIEWS ON ALCOHOL AND ALCOHOLISM

James E. Royce

The Bible condemns drunkenness as evil, yet praises wine as a gift from God. The concept of alcoholism as a disease is of much later origin, and has moral implications on which the churches have varied opinions. Islam forbids alcohol, but Moslem scholars are divided on how much is actually consumed by its followers. Mormons and fundamentalist Protestants are in the same dilemma. The Jews and European Christianity developed viniculture while forbidding drunkenness; American denominations agree on the latter, but differ widely and even vehemently on whether drinking itself is wrong. The WCTU and other movements which led to Prohibition in the U.S. confused abstinence with temperance, creating a false dichotomy between total abstinence and drunkenness which actually negated the concept of temperance. Both Alcoholics Anonymous and various current religious approaches exemplify a rapprochement between theism and the disease model.

Regardless of personal religious beliefs or professed lack thereof, the social scientist is faced with a plethora of facts that illustrate the major influence that the religions of the world have had on the use and misuse of alcohol. These are not only so varied that there is no such thing as "the" religious view on alcohol and alcoholism, but within many of these religious bodies there are paradoxes and discrepancies that make it impossible to categorize their position. Variation in view about alcohol is so great that it is as dangerous to generalize about "all drys" as about "all wets" even when either group happens to be of the same religion.

This is even more true if we widen the field to include other addictive drugs than alcohol. The Hindus and Islam forbid alcohol, but the use of cannabis even in strong forms (hashish) is widespread, as is opium in other nonalcohol-using Oriental societies. Southwest Native American Indians may encourage their children to use peyote in order to dissuade them from alcoholic drinking. As for coffee,

Rev. James E. Royce, S.J., Ph.D., is professor of psychology and Director of the Alcohol Studies Program at Seattle University, Seattle, Washington. He is on the Board of Directors of the National Council on Alcoholism, chairing its committee on religion and alcoholism. His latest book, *Alcohol Problems and Alcoholism: A Comprehensive Survey*, epitomizes his experience as both teacher and counselor in the alcoholism field since 1949. He is a Fellow of the American Psychological Association and past president of APA Division 24 on Philosophical Psychology, the subject of one of his earlier books, entitled *Man and Meaning*.

It was only a few hundred years ago that the devout priests of a certain religious order in Europe protested bitterly against the introduction of coffee at breakfast. They maintained it was expensive, luxurious, worldly, and exotic, not in keeping with religious poverty, and not befitting men dedicated to God. They insisted on retaining their traditional breakfast beverage, which was beer (Ford, 1959:363).

About the only generalization that can be made is that every society has rules about alcohol, usually stemming from religion, but none are standard and none are effective. As we shall see, one of the paradoxes is that the per capita rate of alcoholism among those who drink tends to be higher in the officially "dry" denominations.

Religion and Drinking

Religion has been associated with the use of alcohol since the dawn of history. Isis, goddess of Egypt, is portrayed as promoting beer in 30,000 B.C. A tablet in Babylonia around 6000 B.C. depicts beer being used in religious ceremony (by 4000 B.C. Babylonia had sixteen kinds of beer). The Aztecs and their modern Mexican descendants considered alcohol a gift of the gods. To drink *pulque* was to honor the gods. In Japan, Shinto worship is inseparably entwined with *sake*. We see the use of alcoholic beverages in sacred ceremonial by both ancient and modern Jews, the ancient Greeks and Romans, the Kofyar of Nigeria, and several major Christian denominations. These latter include not only Roman Catholics but also Anglican and Episcopal, Russian and Greek Orthodox, Lutheran, and other sects which have a communion service.

Viktor Frankl talks much of man's basic need for meaning, his concerns with death and guilt, and the modern vacuum of values; Clinebell (1963) discusses possible etiological relations between all this and the psychodynamics of alcoholism. In this view, not all the spiritual problems of alcoholics are merely symptomatic of the deterioration which alcohol has caused, but at least in part may be genuine human problems stemming from basic religious needs.

Moreover, alcohol has been associated not only with religion in the ordinary sense, but also with those extraordinary religious experiences classed as mystical. Even drunkenness has been considered a mystical experience. From the Aztecs with their *pulque* and the rites of Dionysus in ancient Greece to the view of Aldous Huxley about mescaline and the speculations of the psychiatrist Georgia Lolli and the clergyman-psychologist Howard Clinebell about the relation between alcohol use and existential anxiety (meaning of life, fear of death), there is an oft-recurring thread connecting inebriation with God-seeking. St. Augustine says, "O that Thou wouldst enter my heart and inebriate it." A forceful statement is that of William James in his *Varieties of Religious Experience* (1902:378):

The sway of alcohol over mankind is unquestionably due to its power to stimulate the mystical faculties of human nature, usually crushed to earth by the cold facts and dry criticisms of the sober hour....Not through mere perversity do men run after it...the drunken consciousness is one bit of the mystic consciousness.

Although a clergyman, for whom the realm of the supernatural is not foreign, this author, as a clinical psychologist, feels that we must try to keep clear the distinction between the action of a hallucinogenic drug and a true contact with the divinity. Nonetheless, this long history of associating alcohol with religious ecstasy has modern relevance when we see Bill W., co-founder of Alcoholics Anonymous, stating that many alcoholics are "seeking God in a bottle" and that alcoholism is at least in part symptomatic of a desire for mystical experience. It is well known that one of the events in the background history of the founding of Alcoholics Anonymous is the story that Roland H., head of an American chemical company and a "hopeless" alcoholic, went to Zurich for therapy by Carl G. Jung, who told him that he could do nothing for his alcoholism and that his only hope would be an intense religious experience (Kurtz, 1979).

An important aspect of this history is the conclusion of Marshall (1979:454) that socially disruptive drinking occurs only in secular settings, not in sacred or religious contexts. Keller (1970) speculates that one factor in the low rate of alcoholism among Jews may be their use of alcohol in religious ritual after their disassociation with the drunken worship of their Canaanite neighbors. As in the Kava culture we shall mention shortly, it seems historically true that problems occur with alcohol only after it has lost its ritual use.

The Bible

The Bible, highly important in any sociocultural assessment because of the widespread respect for it as a source of belief, has some 687 references to wine, drinking, and drunkenness. Here it is necessary to make a clear distinction between use and misuse. Both in the Old and New Testaments there is clear and consistent condemnation of drunkenness as morally wrong, a sin. The Jews also condemned the Dionysian orgies of their Near East neighbors because they associated them with pagan idolatry. But simply to get drunk, if deliberate (loss of control as a symptom of the disease of alcoholism will be discussed later), in the Judaeo-Christian moral tradition has always been considered to be wrong in itself. Bible commentators usually argue that to deliberately deprive oneself of one's rational control by drink is an attack on that which makes the human person "in the image and likeness of God."

The above consensus on misuse or drunkenness is in striking contrast to the wide and often bitter disagreements among followers of the Bible on the use of wine, as in temperate drinking. In the heat of the American total abstinence movement which was to culminate in Prohibition, zealots tried to argue that whenever "wine" in the Bible was used by Christ or praised as a gift of God, it was really grape juice, and only when it caused drunkenness was it truly wine. The arguments against such an interpretation are formidable. A recent study from a source which could only be presumed *a priori* as biased in favor of the abstinence tradition is *A Biblical Perspective on the Use and Abuse of Alcohol and Other Drugs* by Dr. T. Furman Hewitt, associate professor at Southeastern Baptist Theological Seminary in North Carolina and a graduate of Southern Baptist Seminary (Hewitt, 1980). Yet this scholarly work concurs with the unanimous opinion which I have received from several eminent scriptural scholars: neither the Hebrew nor the biblical Greek word for wine can possibly be interpreted as meaning grape juice, and indeed it is the same wine which Christ drank and which made Noah drunk. The use of wine at the wedding feast of Cana and at the Last Supper are not isolated incidents in Christ's life, but reflect the ordinary lifestyle of His day as seen in the customs of Orthodox Jews down to this time. Science concurs: in a subtropical climate, without refrigeration or preservatives or modern methods of sealing, the natural fermentation process from yeasts on the grape skins or just in the air would make it physically impossible to have grape juice that was not quickly and inevitably wine.

Actually, in spite of its condemnation of drunken misuse, the Bible frequently praises wine and even exhorts its use. "Pure, choice wines" are taken by both the Psalmist and the prophets Amos and Isaiah as signs of God's special love for His chosen people. The "wine that gladdens the heart of man" is to be used also in celebrations of religious and festive joy as well as in more solemn ceremony. St. Paul prescribes wine as medicine (*I Timothy* 5:23, a passage which alcoholics are quick to quote). Abstinence is nowhere in the Bible mandated as a general law, but it is recommended as an ascetical practice for some, or for a short time (e.g., in the Nazarite vow, *Numbers* 6:20).

The early Christian church maintained this biblical tradition of condemning drunkenness but condoning drinking, as exemplified in the writings of Clement of Alexandria, John Chrysostom, Jerome, and Augustine (Raymond, 1927). Churchmen of all ranks imbibed, and wine making became a fine art among the medieval monasteries. Abstinence was sometimes counseled, especially for those who might have a drinking problem or those pursuing a particularly stringent asceticism. Alcohol was used as an anesthetic, although it is a poor one for practical reasons, and this use was accepted as legitimate just as are the drugs used in modern surgery.

Under the Holy Roman Empire, the Church insisted that the civil authorities enforce the temperance law. But the suitability for vineyards was nearly always a major factor in the selection of the site for a new monastery. The Benedictines developed Benedictine and Dom Perignon discovered how to make champagne, while the Carthusians made Chartreuse. Special attention was paid to the proper preparation of Mass wine, but the amount consumed in this ritual use was (and is) minimal and not the source of problems. Most wine and beer was used in connection with meals, becoming the staple drinks with the noon and evening meals of both clergy and laypeople throughout Europe.

The leaders of the Protestant Reformation did nothing to alter this traditional practice. While denouncing drunkenness, they all drank at least temperately, including Luther, Calvin, Knox, and even Wesley, the founder of the Methodists. Calvin, for instance, received an annual stipend in Geneva which included "enough corn and wine for his household" (Parker, 1954:69) and asserted "we are not forbidden to laugh or drink wine" (McNeill, 1954:233). The early American colonists simply transported across the Atlantic this use of beer and wine with meals as a way of life. In both America and Europe, abstinence was voluntary but encouraged, while drunkenness was a sin for Protestants and Catholics alike. But even the Puritans drank; more beer than water was brought over on the *Mayflower*. Beer was served in the dining halls of the Protestant seminaries and in the local parsonage. The Puritan colonial Cotton Mather referred to wine as a "good creature of God."

Prohibition

Total prohibition of all alcoholic beverages was not an idea initiated by the Protestants. The Spartans, the Puritans of ancient times, had limited consumption to a maximum of one pint of wine per day, and the Code of Hammurabi ca. 1900 B.C. was very severe on alcohol abuse. The Aztec, Inca, some Mespotamian, and other ancient cultures show evidence of outright prohibition. The Hindu, Buddhist, and Moslem traditions all forbid alcohol completely. Although alcohol was in the pharmacopoeia of India, prohibition was the rule at one time, and after independence from the British, it was included in the new Indian Constitution (Part IV, art. 47). China had serious problems with drunkenness in the past and legislated prohibition many times. The moral teachings of Confucius on temperance (not abstinence) seem to have prevailed now. Alcohol is not used much outside of meals and is not tied to violence or sexual excess in China, as in many other cultures.

Some authors report that Islamic prohibition came in after the Koran, but others say that the prophet Mohammed himself forbade alcohol as a threat to the unity of his religion, saying that the strong date wine made people "drunk like Christians." In any case the position of alcohol in Muslim society is at best ambiguous. In addition to the condoning of marijuana and its derivatives, there are many reports of heavy alcohol use, especially among some wealthier Muslims who are able to obtain it surreptitiously or travel to nearby jurisdictions where it is not forbidden. In 1971 the first Arab Conference on Alcoholism was held in

Cairo, and in 1975 the International Conference on Alcoholism and Drug Dependence was convened by the Pan Arab Organization of Social Defence and by the Ministry of Health of the State of Bahrain, where it was held. Government officials from fourteen Arab countries attended, and the conference report contains outright disagreement as to the extent of alcohol abuse in Muslim countries (ICAA News, 1976) and the effectiveness of Islam's prohibition—which obviously cannot be 100 percent effective or there would have been no need for the conferences.

Kava ('awa, etc.) is a nonalcoholic intoxicant used in Polynesia and parts of Melanesia and Micronesia made from the pounded root of the pepper tree; *Saukau* on the islands of Ponape and Fiji is similar. Original use seems to have been sacred and ceremonial. Marshall (1976) points out the difficulty of interpreting the various anthropological studies of the Kava culture, but the tragedy seems to have been that what was a highly disciplined, ritualized structure important in their society was destroyed when the white man brought liquor and chaos to the islands. The taboo against alcohol among the Polynesians and Melanesians seems less tied to religion than to fear of losing their sense of direction, among a people who traveled from island to island with no modern navigational aids or even a compass. Later, liquor became both a symbol and a battleground for the Protestant (mostly Calvinistic in orientation) missionaries and still later against the Spanish and German Catholics.

The Protestant movement toward total abstinence and prohibition of all alcoholic beverages seems to have started with the Anabaptists, the so-called third group of the Reformation. They were soon joined by the Friends or Quakers, who were not total abstainers at first. The newly founded Methodist church, the Amish, the Mennonites, and many Congregationalists and Presbyterians sided with them, and later the Pentecostals and most fundamentalist sects, the Seventh-Day Adventists, Christian Science, the Church of Latter-Day Saints (Mormons), and others. The Baptists came to the foreground of the movement, moralizing that all drinking is a sin as is alcoholism itself.

John Wesley and his Methodists were influenced in part by the anti-Baptists and German Pietists, but Calvin was probably the greatest single theological force behind the prohibitionist mentality. The Manichees had solved the problem of evil by postulating two deities, a god of good and a god of evil. As a convert to Christianity from Manicheeism, Augustine showed traces of their thinking in his early and even middle periods: bodily pleasure is bad. It should be noted that Augustine's later writings actually formed the very wording of the Council which condemned Manicheeism, so Calvin's ideas which we now term Puritanical cannot be said to represent Augustine's mature mind (Royce, 1963). How much Calvin was influenced by Augustine is a matter of debate; Calvin was also affected by the ideas current in his turbulent time, his own personal temperament, and Luther's concept of original sin, which was most unflattering to human nature. In any case, he sowed the seeds of prohibition in spite of his own use of wine.

Hence, Puritanism as it flourished in colonial New England is largely the theological descendant of Calvinism and is reflected in the "blue laws" still on the statute books of some New England states, outlawing everything from holding hands in the park to playing cards on Sunday. Jansenism is a Catholic version of Puritanism which developed from Calvinist influence spearheaded by Bishop Cornelius Jansen. In this religious climate where all bodily pleasure is evil, it is not surprising to see the rise of strong moral indignation at the widespread intemperance which had developed in later colonial life and at the glorification of drunkenness on the frontier as a sign of manliness. The prohibition movement may have grown in part out of a genuine concern for the future of the young nation, whose democratic form of government depended on the people keeping their wits intact. But even more it bespoke the Calvinist, Puritan theology common in the colonies, especially in the Presbyterian and Congregationalist churches of New England.

The Calvinist clergyman Lyman Beecher spearheaded the movement, beginning in 1812 with a strong stand for temperance which did not oppose wine and beer but only spirits. By 1825, however, he began advocating total abstinence from all alcoholic beverages. The Temperance Society had become an Abstinence Society by 1836. It lost half its members, but not its momentum. The Good Templars, the Anti-Saloon League, the National Prohibition Party and other groups were formed, especially the Women's Christian Temperance Union (WCTU) in 1874, which completely distorted the issue because the "T" did not stand for temperance but for abstinence, creating confusion in the American mind to this day.

Over these decades of increasingly strident propaganda, the focus shifted from the *abuse* of alcohol or the person misusing it to the substance itself: alcohol became "demon rum" and was to be extirpated from the country. Only the Washingtonian Movement, and later the Salvation Army, showed concern for the *person* affected. To most he was a moral reprobate, a depraved person of weak will who could "reform" if only he willed it.

It is hard for us today to grasp how profoundly this controversy pervaded every facet of American life for a century. Prohibition of alcohol by law became a major issue in every political campaign. In a far smaller population than today's, it is said that the so-called temperance tracts spewed out at a rate of four tons of paper a day. The legend of Carry Nation smashing saloon windows with a hatchet seems exaggerated to us, but it typifies the intense zeal of the prohibitionists and seems to be historical fact, though there is now some question as to her sanity.

The emotional bitterness was matched by conceptual confusion. People failed to distinguish between use and abuse. Temperance was confused with total abstinence, so that many a modern drinker who abhorred drunkenness found himself unwittingly in the camp of its defenders. The two factions polarized the positions and created artificial dichotomies we are still trying to live down. Unfortunately, the Lutherans, Episcopals, Orthodox, Roman Catholics, and Jews, who advocated temperance, were accused of condoning drunkenness because they did not support total abstinence. Paradoxically, the so-called Temperance movement, because it did not allow for temperate drinking as a middle ground between abstinence and intemperance, really negated the whole concept of temperance.

All this religious furor culminated in passage of the Eighteenth Amendment to the U.S. Constitution on January 16, 1920, and its implementation by the Volstead Act. On December 5, 1934, the Twenty-first Amendment repealed the Eighteenth, and the "noble experiment" came to an end. The aftermath is still seen in the divergence of views regarding prohibition among the various churches. Six views may be listed in order of decreasing severity. Some still want to enforce it by law. Others insist on total abstinence as a religious but nonlegal mandate. Thirdly, some churches advocate voluntary abstinence as a norm but do not make it an absolute requirement for being a good Christian, taking a nonjudgmental attitude. A fourth view explicitly recognizes that some good Christians do drink and can do so without harm. Fifthly, there are those who approve moderate drinking except for those whose problems mandate total abstinence; those include the Jews, Lutherans, Orthodox, Anglican or Episcopals, and Roman Catholics. Lastly, there are some permissive, ultraliberal young clergy who are entirely intolerant of any stress on abstinence. Of course, the Jews *require* the use of wine at religious ceremonial, but with an optional use of grape juice.

Disillusionment with prohibition has made it hard for the churches to cooperate. The unwillingness to get involved has resulted in a conspiracy of silence: one reaction to making it the only big problem is to not consider it a problem at all. But the gap is beginning to narrow. In 1968 the United Methodist Church in America relaxed its membership requirement of total abstinence, even though in 1980 it reaffirmed its stand in favor of abstinence as a policy. The Presbyterians have updated their temperance stand, while the Catholics, Lutherans, Episcopalians, and others have urged a serious view of the disease of alcoholism. While some of the Protestant groups have mitigated their rigid stand on abstinence, Catholic thought has shown signs of greater awareness of its necessity for some people. Fr. Theobald Matthew (1790–1856) in Ireland started a "temperance" movement which seems to have been inspired by the Quakers. The Irish Jesuit Father Cullen started the Pioneer Association in 1889, like the "Cercles" in French Catholic Canada advocating total abstinence even for those who do not have a problem, as an example and a prayer for those who do. The first Alcoholics Anonymous group in Europe was formed in Dublin in 1946, and now there are over 150 groups in Ireland.

A major paradox is the finding of researchers that among those who drink, members of "dry" sects tend to have the highest per capita rates of alcoholism.

Snyder (1958) in his study of the Jews noted that those groups who drank most frequently had the lowest rates of alcoholism. Skolnick (1958), Mulford (1964), the Rev. John Keller, and others have observed this concerning some Christian denominations. Lest there be any illusion about the discrepancy between theory and practice, Mulford found that 61 percent of Methodists and 48 percent of Baptists drink; it is estimated that 53 percent of some Fundamentalist sects drink, and the number of Mormons who do so can only be guessed at from the alcohol tax revenue figures in Utah and other evidence that cannot all be written off as due to tourist consumption. Theories as to why "drys" tend to have more alcoholism include greater guilt, lack of physiological immunity because of selective breeding, and lack of disciplined folkways on how to drink moderately. But the fact seems clear, and it confirms from more directly religious-sociological research the failure of prohibition in political history.

Thus we have many paradoxes in the relations between religion and alcohol. Wine is good, but drunkenness is bad. As Jellinek once said, it gladdens the heart but puts to sleep the soul. Is it a creature of God or "demon rum"? Alcoholism came to be seen as a disease, yet the most successful treatment to date is the intensively spiritual program of Alcoholics Anonymous. And AA itself grew out of the failure of a religiously inspired movement, Prohibition.

Moral Issues

As we turn to the moral issues involved, we see more paradoxes. In contrast to the concept of alcoholism as a disease, which favors diminished culpability on the part of the alcoholic ("Don't mind if Joe is a bit cranky today, he's got a bad cold"), the prohibitionists tended to put blame where it is probably least deserved—by condemning the drunkenness of the alcoholic. The alcoholic was seen as a willful sinner, who was urged to use his will power—which to the proponent of the disease model is as vapid as urging a tubercular man not to cough. More recently, the disease concept, which started as nonmoral, is seen by one author (Beauchamp, 1980) as "blaming" the alcoholic rather than society. Ironically, when Marty Mann started the National Council on Alcoholism, with its stress on the disease concept, she put equal stress on society by her insistence that it is a *public* health issue.

Religion is inextricably entwined with these moral problems, but social science throws another light on them by exploring the great variety in drunken behavior in various cultures. Among others, Marshall (1979), Everett *et al.* (1976), and especially MacAndrew (1969) report that even excessive drinking does not always result in the same types of behavior in different societies, for a variety of reasons. In contrast to what we said about the Chinese, in some people, excess leads to disinhibition of sexual and aggressive impulses, which in turn may lead to later guilt in a society where repression is punctuated by abreactive drinking bouts in which the superego is dissolved in alcohol. In cultures where there is less anxiety, excess may lead to more controlled expression of impulses followed by no guilt. In still other tribes, drunken behavior may be a result of conquest by invaders who destroyed a civilized structure, or may be a not-too-subtle protest by way of living *down* to the white man's expectations (Lurie, 1971).

In all this there is a need to keep clearly in mind the distinction between drinking, drunkenness, and alcoholism. Religions have disagreed widely on the morality of drinking, as detailed in the above section on Prohibition. Most religions have agreed in condemning drunkenness, although in some non-Western cultures drunken behavior is allowed under very rigid and controlled conditions. But little has been said about the moral implications of calling alcoholism a disease. The Jesuit moral theologian Ford (1951), Clinebell (1968), and Royce (1981:291–303) are among the few who have explored this latter area. Their conclusions can be summarized as follows.

First to be addressed is the difference between choosing to drink and choosing to be an alcoholic. It is as futile to choose not to be an alcoholic as it is silly to feel guilty about being one; it is simply not a matter of choice. (Attempts at controlled drinking by recovered alcoholics to a large extent ignore this; given the nature of the disease, they are really attempts at choosing not to be an alcoholic.) Before recovery, the alcoholic has little or no choice about drinking; the function of treatment is precisely to restore the ability to choose not to drink.

Calling alcoholism a disease does not eliminate all moral responsibility: the diabetic has an obligation to take insulin and follow a diet, and the alcoholic has at least some choice about accepting treatment or AA or whatever means are necessary to prevent taking that first drink. The alcoholic's diminished freedom of choice, due to the toxic condition, throws more obligation on others and society to demand treatment which, it is hoped, will create the conditions necessary for free choice. After recovery, the alcoholic is still less free than those who have never had this psychophysiological disposition, but most are able to take the necessary means to avoid drinking.

Religion and Alcoholism

Lastly, beyond these moral considerations is the question of what religion has contributed to the treatment and prevention of alcoholism. Since some repressive religions seem to have produced higher rates of alcoholism, one is tempted to conclude that religion has done more to cause than to prevent. Yet, the true temperance seen in other religions suggests that certain religious beliefs and practices can prevent excess. At least, the image of the church formerly associated with the judgmental crusading of the Prohibition era seems to be giving way to a more positive and enlightened approach. Things have moved beyond the old wet-dry moralizing to guidelines on healthy lifestyle, appropriate versus non-appropriate drinking, free choice not to drink in a largely drinking society, and public policy issues which have been dubbed neoprohibition by the liquor industry but are really based on research showing that there is indeed some connection between promotion or availability and abuse (Beauchamp, 1980; Moore and Gerstein, 1981).

In this, the American churches are beginning to take positions and be heard, cooperating with health and social service professions nationally and locally, both governmental and volunteer. Clergymen are learning to look upon Alcoholics Anonymous as complementary rather than competitive to formal religion and to use Al-Anon as a spiritual resource in their family counseling. Positive spiritual values are being substituted for feelings of guilt and punishment, which did little more for the alcoholic than to provide an excuse to drink again. Many clergymen are becoming educated about alcoholism, with the result that they are able to allow and even help recovering alcoholics to grope their way back toward God out of the alcoholic fog, through the general concept of a Higher Power as talked about in Alcoholics Anonymous, waiting for a year or two before they are ready to find God in a denominational or institutional religion.

This trend is not peculiar to current mainstream churches. William Booth, founder of the Salvation Army, had stated in the last century that alcoholism is "clearly a disease" (Booth, 1890:48). The Emmanuel Movement in Boston in 1906 was a church-sponsored psychoreligious clinic which based its approach on the concept of alcoholism as a disease. More recently, the U.S. government has financed shämans as part of a Navajo effort to combat alcoholism through a health restoration program, and the current revival of once-forbidden spirit dances among Pacific Northwest tribes is seen as effective against alcoholism, both as prevention and treatment (Wilek, 1982). Emphasis is on Indian identity, the spiritual, and good health—all of which are vitiated by alcohol.

Psychologists, who were understandably suspicious of religion in the form of revival-meeting emotionalism, are now seriously studying Alcoholics Anonymous in an effort to unravel why it has been numerically the most successful approach to the rehabilitation of alcoholics. If the psychologist is a materialist, the AA member might well reply, "there are more things in heaven and earth than are dreamed of in your philosophy, Horatio." AA is not a religion in the sense of an organized institution with a particular creed, cult, and code. God is always referred to as one's Higher Power, or God as the individual wishes to understand Him. There is great tact in handling the skepticism of the atheist or agnostic and great care not to impose sectarian religion on anyone. But the fact is that AA is an intensely spiritual program. In the Twelve Steps which are its heart, God is mentioned explicitly six times and implicitly twice more. Remove God and it is simply not AA. One may call it natural or philosophical religion as opposed to revealed religion, although the members usually prefer to call it simply "spiritual."

The salient fact is that it is not theory but the actual experience of over a million people, to whom the most important aspect is that it works.

Psychologists have raised the question as to whether this emphasis on God betrays a kind of neurotic dependency or escapism. To this, the AA member would probably reply that if God is the supreme reality, then it is the atheist who is escaping. We are all dependent on oxygen, yet no one considers this admission neurotic. Viktor Frankl tells the story of the woman who saw a stork in the zoo, after being told that the "stork story" was just a myth, to illustrate that in psychotherapy both therapist and patient often uncover the spiritual realities that are in all lives, even those of the avowed atheist. Indeed, AA would see it as the height of egotism to refuse to recognize any higher power than oneself. For AA members, the acceptance of this in practice does not lead to enslavement but to a sense of freedom of choice not to drink. Turning one's life and will over to the care of a loving God does not absolve one from the responsibility of doing one's share, any more than living one day at a time means not buying fire insurance until the day one's house burns down.

In short, the "natural religion" of Alcoholics Anonymous contains a great deal of plain common sense, whatever individual AA members may do with it. While not pretending to be professional therapy, the honest self-examination and confession, the making amends wherever possible, and promptly admitting it when wrong all comprise an authentic encounter comparable to the best in reality therapy. The fellowship and its warm stress on love of God and others is an effective antidote for the loneliness most alcoholics have come to feel. Serenity is sought through humble trust in God rather than from tranquilizers or the bottle. Anxiety, resentments, pride, fear, impatience, and selfishness are never eliminated from most lives, but for the AA member who works the program of the Twelve Steps diligently, these become less of a problem than for many other people (Royce, 1981:283-289). The kind of psychological growth and deep personality change necessary for successful rehabilitation of the alcoholic seems greatly facilitated by a relationship with God, whether achieved through AA or formal religion or both.

REFERENCES

Beauchamp, Dan E.
1980   *Beyond Alcoholism: Alcohol and Public Health Policy.*   Philadelphia: Temple University Press.
Booth, William
1890   *In Darkest England and the Way Out.*   London: International Headquarters of the Salvation Army.

Clinebell, Howard J.
1963   Philosophical-Religious Factors in the Etiology and Treatment of Alcoholism. *Quarterly Journal of Studies on Alcohol* 24:473–488.
Clinebell, Howard J.
1968   *Understanding and Counseling the Alcoholic Through Religion and Psychology.* Rev. ed. Nashville: Abingdon Press.
Everett, Michael W., Jack O. Waddell, and Dwight B. Heath (eds.)
1976   *Cross-Cultural Approaches to the Study of Alcohol: An Interdisciplinary Perspective.* The Hague: Mouton.
Ford, John C.
1951   *Depth Psychology, Morality, and Alcoholism.* Weston: Weston College.
Ford, John C.
1959   Chemical Comfort and Christian Virtue. *American Ecclesiastical Review* 141(6): 361–379.
Hewitt, T. Furman
1980   *A Biblical Perspective on the Use and Abuse of Alcohol and Other Drugs.* Raleigh: North Carolina Department of Human Resources.
ICCA News
1976   Bahrain: Report from the Conference. International Council on Alcohol and Addictions 4(1): 1–11.
James, William
1902   *The Varieties of Religious Experience.* New York: Longmans, Green.
Keller, Mark
1970   The Great Jewish Drink Mystery. *British Journal of Addiction* 64:287–296.
Kurtz, Ernest
1979   *Not-God: A History of Alcoholics Anonymous.* Center City, Minn.: Hazelden.
Lurie, Nancy O.
1971   The World's Oldest On-Going Protest Demonstration: North American Indian Drinking Patterns. *Pacific Historical Review* 40:311–332.
MacAndrew, Craig
1969   *Drunken Comportment: A Social Explanation.* Chicago: Aldine.
Marshall, Mac
1976   A Review and Appraisal of Alcohol and *Kava* Studies In Oceania. In *Cross-Cultural Approaches to the Study of Alcohol*, edited by Everett, M. W., J. O. Waddell, and D. B. Heath, 103–118. The Hague: Mouton.
Marshall, Mac (ed.)
1979   *Beliefs, Behaviors, & Alcoholic Beverages: A Cross-Cultural Survey.* Ann Arbor: University of Michigan Press.
McNeill, John T.
1954   *The History and Character of Calvinism.* New York: Oxford University Press.
Moore, M. H., and D. R. Gerstein (eds.)
1981   *Alcohol and Public Policy: Beyond the Shadow of Prohibition.* Washington: National Academy Press.

Mulford, Harold A.
1964   Drinking and Deviant Drinking, U.S.A., 1963.   *Quarterly Journal of Studies on Alcohol* 25:634–650.
Parker, T. H. L.
1954   *Portrait of Calvin.* Philadelphia: Westminster Press.
Raymond, I. W.
1927   *The Teaching of the Early Church on the Use of Wine and Strong Drink.* New York: Columbia University Press.
Royce, James E.
1963   How Puritanism Persists.   *Insight: Quarterly Review of Religion and Mental Health* 1(3): 3–6.
Royce, James E.
1981   *Alcohol and Alcohol Problems: A Comprehensive Survey.* New York: The Free Press.
Skolnick, Jerome H.
1958   Religious Affiliation and Drinking Behavior.   *Quarterly Journal of Studies on Alcohol* 19:452–470.
Snyder, Charles R.
1958   *Alcohol and the Jews: A Cultural Study of Drinking and Sobriety.* New Haven: Yale Center of Alcohol Studies.
Wilek, W. G.
1982   *Indian Healing: Shämanic Ceremonialism in the Pacific Northwest Today.* Surrey, B. C.: Hancock House.

SOCIAL THOUGHT, CULTURAL BELIEF, AND ALCOHOL

Mac Marshall

American conventional wisdom about the effects of ethanol beverages on drinkers is discussed. It is argued that "rediscovery" of the disease model of alcoholism has coincided with the public "ownership" of alcohol-related problems by physicians. The role medical practitioners have played in establishing and upholding American beliefs about alcohol is discussed, and it is noted that this has prevented other points of view from gaining public attention. This is lamentable since many of the "scientific beliefs" that underlie the medical model do not stand up to scrutiny when the cross-cultural record is examined. The importance of considering psychosocial and cultural factors along with biophysical and medical variables in achieving a complete understanding of the relationship between human beings and alcohol is emphasized.

Whether we drink heavily, moderately, or are totally abstinent, we all possess a host of commonsense understanding concerning the effects of alcohol...however diverse our "source materials" and however fortuitous our actual contacts with them, they have produced a high degree of unanimity among us concerning what we take to be at least certain of the effects of alcohol on man (MacAndrew and Edgerton, 1969:1).

Introduction

MacAndrew and Edgerton (1969) open their highly influential book, *Drunken Comportment*, by highlighting Americans' commonsense understandings about alcohol—what they call the "conventional wisdom" or "what everybody knows." My concern in this paper is to explore American conventional wisdom surrounding alcoholic beverages in more detail. Specifically, I shall focus on general American cultural beliefs about beverage alcohol and what ethanol is believed to do to those who ingest it. Noting Roizen's recent point that, "there may be an important distinction to be drawn between what respondents see as alcohol's effects *in general* and alcohol's effects *on oneself*" (1983:253), I am explicitly concerned with the former set of beliefs.

Mac Marshall received his B.A. from Grinnell College and his M.A. and Ph.D. in anthropology from the University of Washington. Presently, he is Professor and Chairperson of the Department of Anthropology, University of Iowa. His research on alcohol and culture has been conducted in Truk, Micronesia, and as director of a nationwide investigation of alcohol use/abuse for the Papua New Guinea government during 1980–81. He is author of *Weekend Warriors: Alcohol in a Micronesian Culture*, and editor of two compendia: *Beliefs, Behaviors and Alcoholic Beverages: A Cross-Cultural Survey*, and *Through a Glass Darkly: Beer and Modernization in Papua New Guinea*. At the moment he is continuing his analysis of data gathered in Papua New Guinea for publication.

Culture is a basic concept, for anthropologists, to which many different meanings have been attached over the past century (Kroeber and Kluckhohn, 1963). These varied definitions have given the culture concept a certain vagueness, and hence it is necessary to make clear just what is meant by the term in this paper. For at least two decades, a movement has been underway in anthropology to sharpen the meaning of the culture concept and to distinguish it clearly from the concept of society or social behavior (e.g., Geertz, 1973; Goodenough, 1981; Murdock, 1965; Schneider, 1976). In keeping with this recent movement, culture is here defined as a shared, learned, socially transmitted set of orienting beliefs, rules, attitudes, values, and basic premises with which people order and make sense of their experience and of the cosmos.

Anthropologists traditionally have written about small, face-to-face, relatively homogeneous groups of people living in often remote and exotic rural settings. Anthropological field research methods which rely heavily on intensive, longterm participant observation and in-depth interviewing, are said by some to be illsuited to an examination of mass society. But given the anthropological interest in *culture*, as well as society, anthropologists have found it both possible and fruitful to examine the cultural systems of large, urban, complex plural societies like the United States (e.g., Hsu, 1975, 1981; Schneider, 1968; Varenne, 1977).

In this paper, my rather unorthodox approach to American cultural beliefs about alcohol grows out of such research. The discussion to follow is predicated on the assumption that, despite the considerable diversity in values, ideas, and beliefs held by Americans according to their various ethnic, regional, educational, age, and other characteristics, certain overarching beliefs form a dominant cultural paradigm that is shared (or at a bare minimum, recognized) by nearly all Americans. While this paradigm is clearest when contrasted with others of the same order of generality (see, e.g., Hsu, 1981), it informs nearly every American's routine daily experience. The argument, then, is that there is a set of general cultural ideas that characterize "Americanness." From this it follows that there is also a set of general American cultural ideas about the relationships between human beings and alcoholic beverages.

American Cultural Beliefs about Alcohol

Let us begin by summarizing what MacAndrew and Edgerton take the American conventional wisdom about alcohol to be. What they call the "very cornerstone" of what everybody knows about the matter is stated most concisely as follows: "Just as changes in the efficiency with which we exercise our sensorimotor capabilities are consequent upon the action of alcohol on our innards, so too are changes in the manner in which we comport ourselves with our fellows" (1969:11). They contend that Americans believe alcohol to produce two kinds of effects in the bodies of whose who consume it: (a) it affects such sensory functions as motor coordination, reaction time, visual acuity, etc., and (b) alcohol's "toxic assault upon 'the higher brain centers'" makes the drinker "temporarily immune to the action of those internalized constraints ('inhibitions') that normally serve to keep his comportment within proper bounds" (1969:63). The first set of beliefs is said to account for physical changes such as staggering and slurred speech, while the second set of beliefs is said to explain psychological and behavioral changes—particularly changes for the worse.

Beyond this general description of alcohol's presumed effects on our bodies and minds, MacAndrew and Edgerton present a number of more specific American cultural beliefs about booze. They tell us that Americans know that drinking and driving don't mix (1969:1), but "If drinking and driving don't go together, drinking and partying most emphatically do" (1969:3). Americans widely believe alcohol to be a disinhibitor—particularly in regards to behavioral controls over sex and violence. MacAndrew and Edgerton use Ogden Nash's classic aphorism "Candy is dandy, but liquor is quicker" to illustrate the belief that consumption of alcoholic beverages will rapidly reduce "a woman's resistance to a man's amorous advances" (1969:2). Likewise, they tell us that "We all know...that when people drink, the odds are appreciably increased that some unpleasant incident...will ensue" (1969:3).

In addition to these specific American cultural beliefs about alcohol and its effects summarized by MacAndrew and Edgerton, several others will be noted here before we examine where these beliefs originated. Williams mentions that beverage alcohol was included with other substances "believed to increase the vital powers by exciting the circulatory system" in a group of early nineteenth-century medicines labeled "stimulants" (1980:545-547, 549, 555), and many Americans continue to believe that ethanol is a stimulant rather than a sedative, as it is classified by pharmacologists. This belief probably persists because of Americans' association of alcohol with parties, conversation, loquacity, and hilarity. Americans also believe that certain kinds of alcohol are appropriate for certain kinds of people and for certain sorts of occasions. For example, champagne is associated with very special celebrations like weddings or job promotions. A cold beer is appropriate following a hard day's work. Different drinks have the reputation of being "a man's" or "a woman's" drink. The *kind* of alcohol consumed and the *manner* (or mixture) in which it is drunk are believed by most Americans to show something about the social status and self-image of the drinker (compare the remark attributed to Billy Carter that he had a red neck, white socks, and Pabst Blue Ribbon beer.).

Changing Beliefs About Alcohol in America

That American cultural conceptions about alcohol have changed over time has been well documented (e.g., Levine, 1978, 1983; Watts, 1982; Williams, 1980).

These changes in general cultural orientation to alcoholic beverages are important in helping us to understand the current American conventional wisdom about alcohol and its effects.

Levine (1978) has shown that the English colonies in the New World were decidedly "wet" during the seventeenth and eighteenth centuries. Drunkenness was a widespread occurrence, but it was not a social concern. The idea of addiction had not yet been invented: "...drinking was ultimately regarded as something over which the individual had final control. Drunkenness was a choice, albeit a sinful one, which some individuals made" (1978:149). It was in the early nineteenth century that the dominant set of beliefs about alcohol in America underwent a profound shift. Following the work of Dr. Benjamin Rush, the conception of alcohol addiction was developed in which drunkenness was no longer viewed as a matter of free will—the drunkard began to be viewed as someone who had lost control over drinking behavior. Spirituous liquor was identified as the causal agent of a disease condition which we now call alcoholism. Concurrent with this medically inspired paradigm shift came the temperance movement, which, significantly, claimed Benjamin Rush as its founder. Of this fundamental alteration in American beliefs about alcohol, Levine notes that "What was new...was the legitimacy of *a particular way of interpreting the experience and behavior* of drunkards" (1978:154; emphasis added). In other words, a new set of cultural beliefs was gaining ascendancy.

As the nineteenth century unfolded, the temperance movement shifted its concern from broad social reform to Prohibition. The idea of addiction began to occupy a more marginal position, as other "evil effects" of alcohol (e.g., its role in contributing to accidents and family problems) assumed center stage. Levine argues that it was not until the 1930s and 1940s that alcoholism was "rediscovered" as an addiction and a disease, but when this occurred it was a rediscovery with a new twist. Now alcohol was seen as addicting to only some people for reasons unknown but thought to lie in the individuals' genes rather than in the drug *per se*: "The result has been a somewhat 'purer' medical model—that is, there is less of a tendency to view addiction as self-inflicted disease" (Levine, 1978:162).

Williams (1980) also has written of historical changes in Americans' beliefs about alcohol—especially its medicinal role. She observes that beverage alcohol was viewed primarily as a food prior to 1820 and that it formed part of a normal daily diet. At this time in history, it did not have any special status as a medicine; however, "The temperance movement gave it a special place as a powerful substance. Perhaps it is not surprising that alcohol, deprived of its ordinariness and given special powers by the temperance movement, was taken up by physicians as a drug of considerable authority" (1980:564).

Current Beliefs About Alcohol in America

Sahlins (1976) refers to advertising agents (and anthropologists) as "hucksters of the symbol," and he credits advertising agents with having their finger on the pulse of the culture. A successful advertisement must draw on symbolic resources that are widely understood in the culture to create a market for a product. Following this suggestion that advertising might provide special insight into a culture, a brief look will be taken at American alcoholic beverage advertisements to see if they reveal anything about general American beliefs about booze.

Mosher and Wallack assert that advertising creates the impression "that drinking increases sexual prowess; promotes social acceptance and success; insures pleasure without harm; and helps solve personal problems" (1979:89). The burden of their argument is that the reality of drinking—as opposed to this set of positive association—is often quite otherwise.

Breed and DeFoe (1979) analyzed themes in magazine alcohol advertisements and discovered that promises of "desired outcome states" with respect to lifestyle constituted "a fundamental element in alcohol advertising." The major "lifestyle ads" that they identified, in descending order of frequency, were: (1) wealth/prestige/success; (2) approval/acceptance/friendship; (3) relaxation/leisure/carefree; (4) hedonistic pleasure; (5) exotic association/foreign places; (6) individualistic behavior or philosophy; and (7) sex. Beyond this, they discovered that "When people are featured, two interesting patterns suggest how the people relate to the alcohol. In one, the man is fascinated by the drink while the woman is equally fascinated by the man. The other pattern finds the man and woman relating to each other through the alcohol; both are staring thoughtfully at the drink" (1979:519).

According to Marsteller and Karnchanapee (1980), the use of women has been carefully controlled in alcoholic beverage advertising because advertisers and legislators alike believe that sexy ads would increase both beverage sales and undesirable behavior following drinking. Despite this, they chronicle a trend in recent liquor advertisements that equates drinking with romance, glamour, and sexual success (1980:10).

Related to these analyses of advertisements is Finn's (1980) interesting look at attitudes toward drinking as revealed in studio greeting cards. He found that between 4 and 10 percent of the greeting cards in every retail store included in his study treated alcohol themes, with the following five themes recurring over and over again: (1) drunkenness as a concomitant of celebrations; (2) drunkenness as humorous, enjoyable, or harmless; (3) problem drinking and alcoholism as humorous; (4) alcohol as medicinal; and (5) drinking linked with sex.

A set of common themes emerge very clearly from the alcohol advertisements and studio greeting cards. First, alcohol is presented as being linked to social approval, acceptance, friendship, and success. Second, alcohol is presented as promoting harmless—even humorous—hedonistic pleasure as a concomitant of leisure time and celebratory activities. And finally, alcohol is presented as a sexual facilitator, increasing both sexual prowess and sexual success.

A moment's reflection will show that these first two themes are tied directly to that aspect of the conventional wisdom pointed out by MacAndrew and Edgerton, namely, that for Americans, drinking, partying, and "the good times" most emphatically go together. The third theme—that "liquor is quicker"—simply echoes MacAndrew and Edgerton's observations on Americans' belief in the disinhibitory effects of ethanol when it comes to sexual control. So we find, as indeed we do in any cultural tradition, that basic American beliefs about alcohol get repeated and reinforced in many different ways through a kind of cultural redundancy.

American Culture and the "Ownership" of Alcohol

Gusfield has authored an important book that bears on issues being addressed in this paper. In it he develops the concept of "ownership" in reference to public problems like drinking and driving. He defines "ownership" as "the ability to create and influence the public definition of a problem..." (1981:10) and he goes on to observe that

> At any time in a historical period there is a recognition that specific public issues are the legitimate province of specific persons, roles, and offices that can command public attention, trust, and influence. They have credibility while others who attempt to capture public attention do not. Owners can make claims and assertions. They are looked at and reported to by others anxious for definitions and solutions to the problem (1981:10).

Clearly, problem "ownership" also involves control over major cultural beliefs surrounding the problem. The owners "create and influence public definitions" and "can make claims and assertions" to which the public gives credence. It is this aspect of Gusfield's concept of ownership that I shall use to examine general American cultural beliefs about alcohol.

Ownership of public problems means that only certain points of view—certain "versions of reality"—have precedence at any given time and that other ways of viewing the problem are ignored unless or until ownership shifts to another group. The argument will be developed below that contemporary American conventional wisdom about alcohol and its effects is a product of the medicalization of alcoholic beverages and alcoholism which began in the early nineteenth century and gained complete control following Prohibition.

As professional medicine gained ascendance over folk and patent medicine during the nineteenth century, physicians came to be accorded ever greater prestige. With the tremendous advances in the technological and pharmacological armamentarium available to physicians in the twentieth century has come still greater social status and financial remuneration. In America, physicians have become the "high priests" of applied science.

Americans are fond of believing in what they take the "true scientific facts" to be on any given topic (concerning how this has influenced American cultural notions of kinship, see Schneider, 1968:23). From the layperson's point of view, science provides ultimate truth and useable facts rather than current understandings and disposable hypotheses. Thus, a group who can invoke the mystique of science can command attention and capture the public imagination in America, the more so if they already enjoy high prestige for other reasons. This is the case at present with American medical practitioners. They not only "own" alcohol problems; they also legitimize general cultural beliefs about what alcohol is and what it does to people.

Recall that Williams (1980) has documented the influence of the temperance movement on the meaning of alcohol in America. In particular she describes what I would call the "medicalization" of ethanol, in which it was converted from a mundane, everyday victual to a special occasion drug of high potency. Medical doctors were instrumental in bringing about this new definition of beverage alcohol, and medical doctors "by the 1820s and 1830s...were in the vanguard of the antiliquor crusade..." (Williams, 1980:560). Suddenly, this new high potency drug was perceived to be potentially addictive—it was "something special" that "could do things to you" or "make you do things" for which you were not totally responsible because you were *under the influence of a drug.* This redefinition, as we shall see, is crucial for understanding modern American cultural ideas about alcohol and human behavior.

Medical science, with psychiatry at the forefront, has fostered and nurtured the American conventional wisdom that views alcohol as a disinhibitor. MacAndrew and Edgerton (1969:1–12) provide numerous examples of medical definitions that have become public definitions in America, only one of which will be repeated here:

Since *alcohol depresses the powers of judgment,* drinking may *release inhibitions*....As far as sexual behavior is concerned, it is well-known that *alcohol reduces the inhibitions* of individuals and *removes the controls.* The individual becomes careless and will often do things under the influence of alcohol that he would not do if his judgment were not impaired. Therefore, *impairment of the judgment by alcohol may cause sexual behavior* that would not occur were he not exposed to *the loss of control that alcohol brings about* (Block, 1965:219–220; emphasis added).

Make no mistake about it! Alcohol is the cause and the culprit. It impairs and depresses judgment, reduces and releases inhibitions, and brings about loss of control, leading to such things as untoward sexual behavior. According to the medical model, control, judgment, and inhibitions reside in the "higher centers" of the brain. The image is that of a governor—what Freud called the superego—controlling the operation of the human machine so long as the governor is not "turned off" by ethanol. If it is, then watch out! Presumably, anything goes.

Conclusions

Our review of the American conventional wisdom about alcoholic beverages has shown that Americans believe alcohol to have two major kinds of effects on people: physiological and psychological. The psychological changes supposedly wrought by alcohol's toxic assault on the central nervous system often involve disinhibited behavior on the part of the drinker, including potentially disruptive sexual or aggressive behavior. Such behavior is explained and often condoned by Americans as a consequence of the drug's effects on our innards. After all, the owners of the alcohol problem have told us that this is why drinking often leads to disruption. Our doctors have defined the situation for us—they have provided our "source materials"—and we believe our doctors.

The problem with this particular set of cultural beliefs about alcohol has been well known for at least the past fifteen years, since MacAndrew and Edgerton's book appeared. The problem is that when these "scientific beliefs" are held up to scrutiny against the cross-cultural record of how people act before and after they have consumed alcoholic beverages, these "scientific beliefs" do not begin to explain the data. In fact, it becomes very clear that a great deal more is involved than the simple "assault" of a "toxic drug substance" on people's "higher brain centers."

Most of the research that has been conducted by anthropologists interested in alcohol and other drugs in recent years has documented again and again the fundamental importance of cultural learning, social context, and a host of other "psychosocial" factors in achieving a complete understanding of the relationship between *Homo sapiens* and ethanol. I have summed this up elsewhere as follows:

> While ethanol's pharmacological effects cannot be denied they seem to be the least interesting aspect of the human process of getting drunk. The anthropological material suggests that drinking booze is much like having sex, in that the following factors figure prominently in whether the undertaking will prove "successful": presuppositions about what will happen; mood; an appropriate physical and social setting; and the previous experiences

of the active participants (Marshall, 1983:199–200).

So long as the medical model of drunkenness and drunken comportment continues to command the arena of alcohol studies, so long as doctors "own" the problem to the exclusion of other "versions of reality," just so long will Americans offer drunkenness as an excuse for antisocial behavior ranging from rowdiness to wife beating to homicide. And so long as the medical model and the conventional wisdom are one and the same, the laws of the land will continue to provide reduced penalties for those who commit crimes while "under the influence" of alcohol. For, after all, their higher brain centers were inoperative and they did not know what they were doing.

REFERENCES

Block, M. A.
1965   *Alcoholism: Its Facts and Phases.* New York: John Day.
Breed, W., and J. R. DeFoe
1979   Themes in Magazine Alcohol Advertisements: A Critique. *Journal of Drug Issues,* 9(4):511–522.
Finn, P.
1980   Attitudes Toward Drinking Conveyed in Studio Greeting Cards. *American Journal of Public Health* 70(8): 826–829.
Geertz, C.
1973   *The Interpretation of Cultures, Selected Essays by Clifford Geertz.* New York: Basic Books.
Goodenough, W. H.
1981   *Culture, Language and Society.* 2d ed. Menlo Park, Calif.: Cummings.
Gusfield, J. R.
1981   *The Culture of Public Problems: Drinking-Driving and the Symbolic Order.* Chicago: The University of Chicago Press.
Hsu, F. L. K.
1975   "American Core Value and National Character." In *The Nacirema, Readings on American Culture,* edited by J. P. Spradley and M. A. Rynkiewich. Boston: Little, Brown and Co.
1981   *Americans and Chinese: Passage to Differences.* 3d ed. Honolulu: The University Press of Hawaii.
Kroeber, A., and C. Kluckhohn
1963   *Culture.* New York: Vintage Books.
Levine, H. G.
1978   The Discovery of Addiction: Changing Conceptions of Habitual Drunkenness in America. *Journal of Studies on Alcohol,* 39(1): 143-174.

1983   "The Good Creature of God and the Demon Rum: Colonial American and
        19th Century Ideas About Alcohol, Crime, and Accidents." In *Alcohol and
        Disinhibition: Nature and Meaning of the Link*, edited by R. Room and G.
        Collins. NIAAA Research Monograph No. 12. Washington, D.C.: U.S.
        Government Printing Office (DHHS Publication No. (ADM) 82-1246).
MacAndrew, C., and R. B. Edgerton
1969   *Drunken Comportment: A Social Explanation*. Chicago: Aldine.
Marshall, M.
1983   "Four Hundred Rabbits: An Anthropological View of Ethanol as a
        Disinhibitor." In *Alcohol and Disinhibition: Nature and Meaning of the
        Link*, edited by R. Room and G. Collins. NIAAA Research Monograph No.
        12. Washington, D.C.: U.S. Government Printing Office (DHHS
        Publication No. (ADM) 81-1246).
Marsteller, P., and K. Karnchanapee
1980   The Use of Women in the Advertising of Distilled Spirits 1956–1979.
        Journal of Psychedelic Drugs, 12(1): 1–12.
Mosher, J. F., and L. M. Wallack
1979   Proposed Reforms in the Regulations of Alcoholic Beverage Advertising.
        Contemporary Drug Problems, 8(1): 87–106.
Murdock, G. P.
1965   Fundamental Characteristics of Culture. In *Culture and Society, 24 Essays
        by George Peter Murdock*. Pittsburgh: The University of Pittsburgh Press.
Roizen, R.
1983   "Loosening Up: General-Population Views of the Effects of Alcohol." In
        Alcohol and Disinhibition: Nature and Meaning of the Link, edited by R.
        Room and G. Collins. NIAAA Research Monograph No. 12. Washington,
        D.C.: U.S. Government Printing Office (DHHS Publication No. (ADM) 82-
        1246).
Sahlins, M. D.
1976   *Culture and Practical Reason*. Chicago: The University of Chicago Press.
Schneider, D. M.
1968   *American Kinship: A Cultural Account*. Englewood Cliffs, N.J.: Prentice-
        Hall.
1976   "Notes Toward a Theory of Culture." In *Meaning in Anthropology*, edited
        by K. H. Basso and H. A. Selby. Albuquerque: The University of New
        Mexico Press.
Varenne, H.
1977   *Americans Together: Structured Diversity in a Midwestern Town*. New
        York: Teachers College Press.
Watts, T. D.
1982   Three Traditions in Social Thought on Alcoholism. *The International
        Journal of the Addictions* 17(7): 1231–1239.

Williams, S. E.
1980 The Use of Beverage Alcohol as Medicine, 1790–1860. *Journal of Studies on Alcohol* 41(5): 543–566.

SOCIAL THOUGHT IN THE TWENTIETH CENTURY AS IT RELATES TO RESEARCH ON WOMEN, ALCOHOL, AND ALCOHOLISM

Penny Clemmons, Ph.D.

The purpose of this paper is to investigate the relationship between the published research on women and alcohol/ism in the twentieth century and correlative social issues. As our knowledge of women's issues increases, it becomes more and more apparent that substantive data has been ignored and/or neglected in the analysis and critique of social thought as it applies to the research available on women and alcohol/ism.

One problem of research is to study a phenomenon in a broad enough context to be able to apply and generalize the findings in a useful way and not simply add another ream of paper to the ever increasing number of published studies. As research about women and alcohol/ism increased in the 1960s and the early 1970s, results were contradictory, the only available comparison samples were male alcoholics or female psychiatric patients, and there was little comparison or integration of findings. Two consistent statements were repeatedly cited: "while little research is available" and "further research about women needs to be undertaken before...." This state of affairs in available publications led the author to several questions about the existing research on women and alcohol/ism and alcohol use and abuse: What are the parameters of the literature? How many studies have been published? Where are they published? Who are the authors? What is being studied? Why? Is there a historical context? And finally, are there operant social issues which correlate with these studies?

Since social issues, incidence, treatment, psychopathology, drinking patterns, research, social policy, and other variables of women and alcohol/ism have been studied consistently in isolation from each other, any conclusions reached are only of partial significance. A comprehensive approach is needed which will address these aspects of alcohol/ism and women in relationship to one another rather than as individual isolates. Social issues generally remain embedded in the discussion of women and alcohol/ism, and explicit attention is required if we are to provide a more integrative view of alcohol studies.

Penny Clemmons, Ph.D., Coordinator, Clinical Certificate Program in Chemical Dependency, Antioch University, Santa Barbara, California, is a licensed clinical psychologist in private practice; she has presented and published papers in the field of substance abuse. She is a member of Associates for Interdisciplinary Studies, California State Psychological Association, and the National Association for the Advancement of Psychoanalysis. Dr. Clemmons is an NAAP certified psychoanalyst and a licensed marriage, family, and child counselor.

One solution to the problem may be found in the discipline of psychoanalysis. Freud constructed a model defining psychoanalysis as a method of research, a theory of personality, and a modality of treatment. If we approach alcohol studies from this tripartite model, we can gain a holistic view of the field. This paper attempts to build a bridge between individual research studies and relevant and identifiable social issues of this century.

Methodology

Since the data from the research project did not lend itself to rigorous statistical treatment, it was examined from a phenomenological perspective, and the phenomenological method was used to reduce the data to specific themes. All accessible studies on women and alcohol were reviewed. References were obtained from *Psychology Abstracts*, numerous bibliographies, and computer searches. In all, 188 articles were reviewed for the compilation of this article. As books were more difficult to identify, locate, and access, the search was mainly limited to journals. While every effort was made to be all-inclusive, the author is well aware that studies may have been inadvertently overlooked. One problem in reviewing the literature is that journal titles and abstracts do not always accurately reflect the content. There are studies in the literature which deal with women and alcohol but are not identifiable as such. While the accompanying bibliography is one of the most comprehensive compiled on the subject, it is not exhaustive.

Historical Perspective

A review of the literature indicates that the first published research studies on women and alcohol/ism date back to 1937 in *The Journal of Nervous and Mental Disease*. This led the author to examine the social and historical conditions which preceded this new focus in the psychiatric literature.

It is necessary to return to the colonial days to explore the original social context of alcohol in women's lives in the United States. (Unfortunately, it is beyond the scope of this study to explore the role of alcohol and its use in the lives of Native American women.) For the pioneer women, and in particular widows, a common and respected occupation was that of innkeeper or tavernkeeper. This profession was seen as an extension of her vocation as homemaker, housekeeper, and vittles provider and therefore socially acceptable. Women could own inns and taverns but were prohibited in some states from pouring alcohol for public consumption or sale. In these instances, men were hired to tend to the bar.

Throughout the 1700s and 1800s women were encouraged by physicians to use alcohol for medicinal purposes, and nursing mothers were advised to partake of brandy and beer for their health. Patent medicines became popular remedies for various maladies, and their use by women was socially accepted. The alcohol content of these preparations was not publicly acknowledged by the manufacturers, however. Public drunkenness in women was considered an outrage, but there was general acceptance of alcohol use by women except in those religious sects which prohibited alcohol consumption.

Toward the late 1800s the Woman's Christian Temperance Union became a powerful social force in the United States. The leaders were committed to several issues: fair labor laws, the right of women to vote, and the prohibition of alcohol. The Union organized women and provided them with cognitive and emotional reasons to rally. In their Temperance movement women could "legitimately" apply their intellectual prowess, step into the world from the shadows of their homes, and be effective workers and leaders with church support. It was a morally sanctioned volunteer endeavor.

A common problem for women of this era, not unlike today, was the alcoholic husband. Through its support of prohibition, the Union appeared to provide a means to combat this problem. Intervention was unheard of in this time; divorce was socially unacceptable, and women were unlikely to receive the necessary financial, spiritual, or emotional support to provide for themselves or their children. For many, prohibition appeared to be the only solution to the problem.

The impact of the WCTU on women's rights was significant and prophetic of changes to come. Hand in hand with the passing of the Volstead Act in 1919 came the right of women to vote in 1920.

The beginning of the twentieth century was a time of radical change. The war efforts, the decline of Victorian mores, the introduction of Freud's ideas on sexuality, and the utilization of "modern" methods of contraception increased women's social independence. Standards for women were relaxed, compared to previous centuries, and the stage was set for the contemporary woman who could relate to herself, family, and society in new and complex roles. This woman could vote, hold public office, drive a vehicle, divorce, pursue a career, and practice birth control. With the repeal of the Volstead Act in 1933, she could also legally drink.

American society was not prepared to meet the needs of the twentieth century woman or to recognize that she would be privy to some of the same problems as men. Women's capacity to bear children has always set her apart, and with that privilege has come the burden of living with an imposed double standard. Our society suspects anything new or different and frequently equates such occurrence with pathologies and aberrations. As we examine the literature on women and alcohol/ism, we will discover this phenomena.

With this background in mind, the available literature will be examined, reviewed, and critiqued decade by decade, beginning with the 1930s.

1930s

A recurrent theme in the literature is the individual psychopathology of the female alcoholic, which dates back to our earliest studies. The study of alcoholism and women in the 1930s was confined to the domain of psychiatry. Two articles of significance were published in this decade. Wall (1937) studied a population of fifty female alcoholics and compared them to one hundred male alcoholics. The women were observed to have more psychotic pathology than the men and to have more specific disturbances in contrast to the men, who were more similar as a group.

Acute alcoholic hallucinosis in women was studied by Curran (1937). Women were compared to men and found to have heterosexual accusations in their hallucinations while men were found to have homosexual accusations.

A major component in each study was the correlation of pathological narcissism with alcoholism. The diagnosis of alcoholism was considered to be more deviant in women than in men.

1940s

The popular population of female alcoholics to study continued to be the institutionalized state hospital patients. It is not surprising, then, that the predominant theme of these studies continued to be individual psychopathology. Throughout this decade, problem drinking was associated with men; in women it was seen as a symptom of a more serious disorder rather than a problem in and of itself. Psychiatric profiles of the individual female dipsomaniac emphasized her narcissistic oral needs, resentments, and guilt.

Normal or social drinking in women did not become a publishable research interest until the late 1940s. Hecht (1948) studied the incidence of drinking in 336 college women. While 26.8 percent of his sample drank regularly, 13.4 percent were abstainers.

Further studies focused on normative drinking behavior among women in general. Principal investigators in this area were Riley, Marden, and Lifshitz (1948), who studied 791 women who drank alcohol. In comparing this sample with men who drank, they found that women were more likely to drink in the interest of being sociable; men drank for more individual reasons.

Articles specifically about women began to appear in the *Quarterly Journal of Alcohol Studies* in 1948. This journal accounts for more than 25 percent of all published research on women. It provided a major arena for researchers to present their findings about alcoholism in general and women in particular.

The major social issue of the 1940s was World War II. The war effort led to further emancipation of women and acceptance of their unique contribution at home and abroad. It is not coincidental that the first studies of normal drinking in women followed the war; women had "earned" the right to drink, and incidence of drinking in women was a legitimate research interest.

1950s

Prevalence and incidence studies were prominent in this decade, although conflicting evidence was found among Block (1952), Keller and Efron (1955), and Lemere, O'Hollaren, and Maxwell (1956). Block proposed that the incidence of alcoholism in women was as frequent as in men. While other researchers disagreed, this study emphasized the need for equal concern about drinking whether it was by men or women. The significance of this occurrence was that it began to move female alcoholism out of the realm of the pathological and into the realm of physical and social problems.

The effect of physiology on female alcoholism was suggested by Lolli (1953). He hypothesized that menstruation as well as menopause could precipitate uncontrolled drinking. Further investigations of these phenomena have continued up to the present-day studies on premenstrual syndrome. Considerable attention has also continued to focus on the similarities and differences between men and women. Many studies of women appeared to be made acceptable by this comparison.

The literature of this decade is summarized in an article by Lisansky (Gomberg) (1958). Her commitment to the study of female alcoholism from a social scientific perspective has been a significant contribution to alcohol studies, and her work has served as a model for other researchers. The foci of this decade were psychopathology, precipitating circumstances, physiology, incidence studies, socioeconomic background, social class, marital disruption, and drinking patterns.

A clear shift was made in this decade from the individual psychopathology model of earlier times to a social model with a magnitude of variables which needed to be researched. While women were still viewed as deviant for drinking alcohol, new viewpoints were being espoused and studied.

1960s

At least forty-four articles were published from 1960 to 1969, more than double the number published in the two preceding decades, 1939–1959. These studies were concerned with drinking patterns, social variables, treatment, premenstrual tension, prisoners, and demographics. Some of the more prolific authors were Glatt, Karp, deLint, Knupfer, Curlee, Winokur, and, of course, Schukit. While space does not permit an extensive review, some highlights will be noted.

Two classic books were written during this decade: *The Female Alcoholic: A Social Psychological Study*, Kinsey, (1966) and *An American Woman and Alcohol*, Kent, (1967). Both of these books informed the professional community and the lay community that there was a problem that had been ignored. Not long after these publications were available, articles began to appear in women's magazines and periodicals.

In 1969 Curlee postulated the empty nest syndrome as an important variable associated with the woman alcoholic. Housewifery and premenstrual syndrome were also studied as possible antecedents of female drinking.

A new area of interest in the literature was treatment. Studies focused on prisoners, the married, the unmarried, group therapy, individual therapy, outcome, and identification of different types of alcoholism. Psychopathology was still a major emphasis and, in particular, studies investigating the relationship between alcoholism and primary affective illness. As in the late 1950s, social variables were of significant interest: birth order, family history, and parental deprivation were the variables most frequently examined.

Since the social issues of the 1960s and the 1970s are inexorably linked, they will be discussed after summarizing the literature from 1970 to 1979.

1970s

Publication of studies on women and alcohol continued to peak until 1974, when 21 articles were published; over 126 studies are accounted for in the literature in the period 1970–1979. After 1974, however, research began to decline with each succeeding year, with the exception of 1978. There was a wide variation in themes, including many aspects of treatment, theory, and research.

Two predominant themes require our attention: sexual promiscuity and fetal alcohol syndrome. Each of these topics have led to moral censure of the female alcoholic rather than investigation of a social issue. As mentioned earlier, women, because of their capacity to bear children, are treated differently from men. They are the perpetuators of the race. Throughout history, alcohol use in women has been correlated with promiscuity and sexual immorality. Because she bears children, a woman's virtue had to be "protected." Perhaps this was the same reason some states would not allow her to pour liquor in her own business establishment. The popular myth was that while under the influence of alcohol, a woman would consent to or commit sexual acts she would not participate in if sober. This double standard was never applied to men. There's never been an association between male drinking and moral misconduct; frequently male drunkenness is a source of comedy to the observer. In addition to bearing the burden of an alcohol problem, a woman was confronted with society's scorn for her alleged moral turpitude. The first hard data to contradict these suppositions was provided by Schukit (1972) who found that 95 percent of alcoholic women experienced a *decrease* in sexual activity with the use of alcohol.

Further moral censure of the female alcoholic came from recognition of the fetal alcohol syndrome. Attention was focused away from the alcoholic woman and onto her offspring. Identification of this disorder led to continued disparagement of the woman for neglect of the unborn child, rather than increased understanding of the physical ravages of alcohol abuse on both mother and child. Female alcoholism again became a moral issue rather than a sociomedical problem in need of comprehensive treatment. Little attention was given to the emotional concomitants of bearing a child with fetal alcohol syndrome. Since the alcoholic woman "brought these problems on herself," her welfare and well-being were not of primary concern. As is frequently the case, concern about this woman is focused on what she does rather than who she is. The concern is for her effect on society in a moral arena or a maternal arena; it is not the woman as person who is valued but rather the role she is fulfilling for society.

The major social issue of the 1960s and the 1970s was the women's liberation movement and its impact on the quality of life for women in the United States. The feminist movement can be seen as taking up where the WCTU and the Suffragists stopped. Several wars later, women have restructured their role in society and begun to take the positions of equality for which the groundwork had been laid long ago. While many strides were made during this time, there was also a backlash effect. Increased awareness of problem drinking in women was attributed to women's inability to cope with role diffusion. Grandmother's use of patent medicines was no more recognized as substance abuse than the housewife's medicinal prescription for nerves, but the public use of alcohol by "liberated women" was seen as symptomatic of her inability to deal with stress. Acknowledgement of an alcohol problem led to insinuation of more serious problems. Despite the courageous public statements of women like Betty Ford, Jan Clayton, Mercedes McCambridge, and countless others, the stigma of the 1930s still remained.

In 1976 women and alcoholism entered the political arena. Congressional hearings on the status of women and alcohol were held. Subsequent funding cutbacks, however, severely weakened any gains that were made earlier in the decade, and the economic difficulties of the latter years led to severe budgetary constraints. What began as the decade of the female alcoholic began to sputter, and innovative and creative proposals were severely cut or eliminated. Women's projects no longer had priority funding, and the subsequent decline in studies is evident since 1975.

1980s

What social issues can be forecast for this decade, and what effect will they have on research on women and alcohol/ism? This article was first conceived and written in the spring of 1983. At that time there were two prominent issues, one national and one international. In the United States, the economic crisis dominated all sectors of society, and worldwide, the threat of nuclear war by one of the superpowers was the most overriding social issue. The economics of the 1970s led to less and less research as universities, hospitals, and social service agencies all faced substantial cutbacks. Grants became rare commodities and, where available, have been insufficient to fund comprehensive proposals. Despite this dismal outlook, new researchers have emerged who are independent scholars, unaffiliated with a university or hospital. By choice or design, they practice their profession independent of major funding sources, academic support, and political constraints. These truly free scholars, many of whom are women, may hold the key to future research, particularly in the unpopular field of women and alcohol/ism.

The revision of this chapter took place in mid-1985. On the domestic scene, we have entered into another age of prosperity; the economic crisis of the early 1980s is over. Interest rates are plummeting, and the economic forecast is optimistic.

The two major themes that predominate the mid-1980s are violence and drug abuse; for some, the two are inexorably related. For others, the focus is public awareness of our national drug problem. Whether this renewed interest and concern will lead to funding of prevention, treatment, and research in chemical dependency remains to be seen.

As we live through the eighties, the threat of nuclear holocaust continues to be omnipresent. Professionals from varied disciplines have gathered together to protest the irresponsible stockpiling and threatened use of nuclear warfare. Social scientists have begun to study the effects of living under the constant threat of nuclear annihilation on both children and adults. The impact of this issue on alcohol studies is unknown, but it seems that through political necessity our interests will turn from issues of individual psychopathology to issues of global survival. The moralism of past decades appears to be giving way to cooperative efforts to establish peace.

Summary

This paper has investigated the relationship of social issues to the evolution of research on women and alcoholism. It has attempted to bridge the gap resulting from the isolationist view of alcohol studies and to introduce an interdisciplinary approach to the examination of relevant alcoholism research and corresponding social issues. Representative studies of identifiable themes in the literature on women and alcohol have been reviewed in a social-historical context. A by-product of this study was the compilation of a bibliography of studies pertaining to women and alcohol from 1937 through 1979.

REFERENCES

Block, M.
  1952   Alcoholism: The physicians duty. *General Practitioner* 6: 53–58.
Curlee, J.
  1969   Alcoholism and the empty nest. *Bulletin of the Menninger Clinic* 33: 165–272.

Curran, F.
1937   Personality studies in alcoholic women.   *The Journal of Nervous and Mental Disease* 86: 645–667.
Hecht, C.
1948   Drinking and dating habits of 336 college women in a coeducational institution. *Quarterly Journal of Studies on Alcohol* 9: 353–362.
Keller, M., and V. Efron
1955   The prevalence of alcoholism. *Quarterly Journal of Studies on Alcohol* 16: 619–644.
Kent, P.
1967   *An American Woman and Alcohol.* New York: Holt, Rinehart, & Winston.
Kinsey, B.
1966   *The Female Alcoholic: A Social Psychological Study.* Springfield, Ill.: Thomas.
Lemere, F., P. O'Halloran, and M. Maxwell
1956   Sex ratio of alcoholic patients treated over a 20-year period. *Quarterly Journal of Studies on Alcohol* 17: 437–442.
Lisansky, E.
1958   The woman alcoholic. *Annals of the American Academy of Political and Social Science* 325: 73–81.
Lolli, G.
1953   Alcoholism in women. *Connecticut Review of Alcoholism* 5: 9–11.
Riley, J., C. Marden, and M. Lifshitz
1948   The motivational pattern of drinking. *Quarterly Journal of Studies on Alcohol* 9: 353–362.
Schukit, M.
1972   Sexual disturbance in the woman alcoholic. *Medical Aspects of Human Sexuality* 6: 44–65.
Wall, J.
1937   A study of alcoholism in women. *The American Journal of Psychiatry* 93: 943–952.

PROGRESSIVISM AND DRINK: THE SOCIAL AND PHOTOGRAPHIC INVESTIGATIONS OF JOHN JAMES McCOOK

David T. Courtwright
Shelby Miller

John James McCook was a clergyman-turned-reformer who wrote and lectured extensively on alcohol, poverty, and kindred social problems during 1890–1924. He sought to show statistically, photographically, and anecdotally that alcohol generated massive social costs and was therefore a fit object for strict regulation—but not necessarily prohibition. McCook thought drunkenness reprehensible, although he occasionally borrowed concepts and terminology from the inebriety movement, which held that alcoholism was a manifestation of mental disease.

This article describes McCook's investigations, his developing thought on alcohol and alcoholism, and his views on alcohol policy, and relates them to the larger intellectual currents of progressivism, as well as his individual circumstances. A representative thinker in a transitional age, McCook mirrors the many and often contradictory ideas Americans have entertained about alcohol during the last hundred years.

Introduction

The idea that alcohol is directly or indirectly responsible for social ills is an old one and has been systematically pursued in the United States since the 1820s (Aaron and Musto, 1973:142–143). It was not until the turn of the century, however, that reformers were able to demonstrate, in a seemingly scientific way, the myriad costs of drinking and chronic drunkenness. The evidence they assembled constituted a quantum addition to social knowledge on alcohol, and was instrumental in persuading Americans, especially middle-class Progressives, to support prohibition (Timberlake, 1966).

David Courtwright is chairman of the Department of History at the University of Hartford and Assistant Clinical Professor in the Department of Community Medicine at the University of Connecticut Health Center. He received his Ph.D. in History from Rice University. He has published *Dark Paradise: Opiate Addiction in America before 1940* (Harvard University Press, 1982), and other works.
Shelby Miller is a professional librarian at the University of Hartford. She received her M.S. from Louisiana State University. She has done extensive research in the McCook MSS., especially among the photographic evidence.
The authors wish to thank the staffs of the Connecticut Historical Society and the Watkinson Library, Trinity College, for their assistance and the use of their facilities. Permission to reproduce all photographs was granted by The Antiquarian and Landmarks Society, Inc. All photographs are from the Butler-McCook Homestead Collection, Hartford, Connecticut.

Perhaps more than any other figure, John James McCook (1843–1927) embodies the Progressive determination to document the social burden of drinking. McCook was an indefatigable investigator (his collected social reform papers run to fourteen microfilm rolls) who broadcast his findings through lectures, reports, and articles in popular and social scientific journals. Although the practical effect of his researches was to furnish ammunition for the prohibitionists, McCook did not personally favor that remedy. The measures he advocated, however, including a restricted supply of alcohol and the institutionalization and disfranchisement of alcoholics, manifest, in other ways, the basic Progressive impulse for control.

Background and Personality

McCook's career reflects—in fact, virtually caricatures—progressivism as a movement dominated by middle-class professionals (Wiebe, 1967). By the time he launched his social investigations in the 1890s, McCook had been exposed to no fewer than four professions: law, medicine, divinity, and college teaching. Although his intellectual capacities were considerable, it appears that McCook came by such breadth accidentally, as a by-product of a checkered and anxious early career.

McCook, the fifth son and sixth child of John McCook, a country physician, and Catherine Julia Sheldon McCook, was born on February 2, 1843, in New Lisbon, Ohio. His upbringing may be briefly described as respectable and Presbyterian. Even cards were taboo in his family. "With 'religious' people, I came near saying respectable people," McCook recalled years later, "card playing was in the catalogue of vices, along with whiskey drinking, horse racing and other things still more reprehensible. To this day...there is something to me really not quite right about the very glint of a card...." (*The Social Reform Papers of John James McCook*, 1977 [hereinafter SRP]: Roll 7, Frame 663; see also Boyer, 1978:197).

In 1858 McCook entered Jefferson College in Cannonsburg, Pennsylvania, only to be dismissed two years later for editing a "foolish" lampoon the faculty judged to be libelous. He read law in Steubenville, Ohio, until early 1861, when he resolved to set Blackstone aside for the Bible. But the war interrupted his plans for the ministry, and he promptly enlisted when Lincoln issued his first call for volunteers. He was not alone. Altogether, fifteen McCooks, including his father, uncle, four brothers, and eight cousins, fought for the Union; four were killed, three were wounded, and five attained the rank of general officer. So distinguished was the family's war record that it earned the monicker "the fighting McCooks." There is a small irony here, for McCook's paternal grandfather, a Scotch-Irish émigré, joined the Whiskey Rebellion in western Pennsylvania almost as soon as he arrived in the United States (P. McCook, 1964:10). It appears that his descendants were inclined toward neither whiskey nor rebellion.

McCook's army service was brief; after ninety days his regiment was mustered out, and he did not reenlist. He had planned to do so, but his father, concerned about his youth, urged him to return to college instead. With mixed feelings, he enrolled at Trinity College, Hartford, Connecticut, in October 1861. He chose Trinity at the behest of an aunt and orphaned cousin, Eliza Sheldon Butler, who offered to share their house in Hartford.

Eliza Butler, with whom he fell in love, was Episcopalian, as was Trinity College. Impressed by the Episcopal liturgy and *The Book of Common Prayer*, McCook began to consider the priesthood. But he was torn: his roots were Presbyterian, and his initial calling had been in that direction. Unable to resolve his dilemma, he decided, after graduating from Trinity in 1863, to attend the College of Physicians and Surgeons in New York City. But then, in February 1864, he "felt irresistibly drawn to the sacred ministry & abruptly left N.Y." for the Berkeley (Episcopal) Divinity School in Middletown, Connecticut (SRP: Roll 7, Frame 577).

In 1866 he was ordained a deacon, married Eliza Butler, and became rector of St. John's in East Hartford, a parish he would serve, with but brief interruptions, for over fifty years. The following year, 1867, he was ordained a priest. In spite of a growing family—he and Eliza were to have eight children—McCook offered his priestly services *gratis*. But when a serious financial reversal, in the form of peculation by his wife's guardian, afflicted the family, he had to seek salaried income. This he earned by teaching modern languages at his *alma mater*, Trinity College, first as instructor, eventually as full professor and head of the department. His linguistic gifts were remarkable: he was fluent in French and German, proficient in Italian and Spanish, and had a working knowledge of half a dozen other modern languages, not to mention expertise in Hebrew, Latin, and Greek (P. McCook, 1964:16–17).

Four points in this brief sketch are worth elaborating, because they have an important bearing on McCook's later work. First, he was by choice high church; thus, he had no theological predisposition to view alcohol as evil in itself, whatever negative associations may have lingered from his childhood. Second, his personal struggle over the Presbyterian ministry versus the Episcopal priesthood left him with an understanding and toleration of religious differences. McCook preached ecumenicalism, invited all nationalities and creeds to his services, and lived in a multiethnic neighborhood (J. McCook, 1901:14–17; P. McCook, 1964:15, 18–19). Nativism, therefore, will not suffice as a motive for his critical investigations. Third, his experience with medicine and law made him aware of the importance of dispassionate observation and analysis. Although his writings on alcohol-related problems were frequently overlaid with a veneer of judgmental prose, at their core was always an argument, usually statistical in nature. McCook had the heart of a clergyman but the head of a social scientist, a duality apparent in both his published and unpublished papers. Finally, McCook was a cosmopolitan, well-travelled, and fluent in modern languages. The titles in his library show that he kept abreast of overseas developments and that he was inclined to view alcoholism, poverty, and other issues from an international or comparative perspective. In this, certainly, he was decades ahead of most contemporaries.[1]

The Social and Photographic Investigations

McCook's career as a reformer began when he read that Hartford's proposed budget for 1890–1891 included $40,000 for outdoor alms, or aid to the noninstitutionalized poor. Yet, at the same time, New Haven, a city with 30,000 more residents, spent only $15,000 on outdoor relief. Alarmed by these unaccountable differences, citizen McCook dropped his daily paper, jammed on his hat, and marched off to city hall. A town meeting was in progress and McCook offered a budget amendment, hastily scrawled on the back of an envelope, that outdoor alms in Hartford should be held to $15,000. The proposal was debated and a compromise appropriation of $25,000 agreed upon. Then the meeting authorized the creation of a special committee of five to look into the matter and report back to the town selectmen. McCook was subsequently made chairman of the committee, or, as he wryly put it, "the citizen who had brought the Town into the trouble was the first name on the list" (SRP: Roll 1, Frame 103).

McCook took his responsibility seriously. Under his direction the committee, including a journalist, merchant, lawyer, and insurance executive, collected and assimilated a large amount of statistical material. Exceeding the bounds of their original charge, they studied virtually every aspect of alms administration, which they came to see as an interlocking system. Their premise, borrowed from Benjamin Franklin, was that "the best way of doing good to the poor is not making them easy in poverty, but leading or driving them out of it." To accomplish this, outdoor relief had to be more strictly limited. If groceries, rent assistance, and home medical care were generally unavailable, then the poor would face a stark, but fiscally useful, choice: find work or enter the almshouse. Presumably those who chose the latter would be the genuinely destitute, worthy of municipal assistance.

When McCook's committee turned its attention to the almshouse, however, it discovered a disconcerting fact: most of the inmates were, by the standards of the day, decidedly unworthy. They were drunkards and criminals, part of a floating population that drifted in and out of the almshouse as weather and health dictated. McCook, who wrote the committee's final report, described the situation vividly:

They present themselves, or are brought, not infrequently ragged, filthy, shoeless, shivering with incipient delirium, at the office of the selectmen, receive a card and are transported to the almshouse. Then they are bathed, clad in a new suit, if necessary sent to the Infirmary, carefully nursed out of their delirium, fed when convalescent upon whisky and milk. A few days' work follow—prolonged into weeks, perhaps, if it be mid-winter; only a few of those who can get away staying during the summer. The work, otherwise beyond their impaired forces, is made bearable, it may be, by the occasional administration of stimulants....Presently—and it is never long delayed—comes the drawing towards the old life; there is nothing to restrain them; and suddenly the bird has flown. Almost before his absence has been well noted he is back again. The new suit has been pawned, or reduced to rags and filth by a two or three days' debauch, and there follows, bath, a second suit, more whisky and milk, a feeble attempt at work, another flight, another debauch, a third application for ticket at the Halls of Record,—and so on, in a vicious circle as unending as the patience of the first selectman and the indifference of the Hartford taxpayer (McCook, 1891:xlv-xlvi).

McCook went on to calculate that each recidivist cost the city an average of five dollars a week in direct and indirect expenditures. Of the source of this outrage he had no doubt. "The question of alms in Hartford," he wrote, "is largely the question of drink" (McCook, 1891:liv). Drunken paupers and criminals were found, not only in the almshouse, but in city hospital beds, asylums, and in families receiving outdoor relief. The best thing was to sentence them, upon third conviction, to lengthy or indefinite terms in special workhouses, where they would be kept off the streets and forced to earn their keep.

These were harsh judgments, but not atypical. Americans of McCook's class and generation were obsessed with the distinction between the worthy and unworthy poor; millions might be promptly raised for victims of the Chicago fire, but woe betide those improvident enough to disburse coin to able-bodied idlers (Bremner, 1980). The antipathy toward alcoholics in the alms report may also have been a conscious or unconscious expression of McCook's financial anxieties; a man struggling to maintain a large family's standard of living is unlikely to look kindly upon those whose conduct increases his tax bill. But he was not closed-minded. Although he would remain preoccupied with the social burden of drink, McCook nonetheless came to understand that alcoholism was more than a vice, that it was also a complex and in some ways an environmentally determined phenomenon.

Three evolving views were the product of further research. In essence, McCook was willing to pursue his investigations because he felt he was making progress. The 1891 alms report was widely praised and its recommendations adopted *in toto*. Relief expenditures declined and the report, of which 6,000 copies were printed, became a model for efficient municipal charity (SRP: Roll 1,

Frames 105–111). McCook was appointed to a second committee, this one to explore possible changes in Connecticut's penal laws, and was much in demand as a lecturer on the itinerant poor and other social problems. To adequately discharge these responsibilities, he felt he had to gather more information on a wide variety of topics.

His first project was a survey of "casual lodgers or tramps." In November 1891, he sent questionnaire blanks to the mayors of forty cities, with the request that they be passed on to authorities in charitable or penal institutions where tramps were housed. He received information on 1,349 cases from fourteen cities. McCook minded this data heavily, referring to it often in subsequent articles. Of particular interest here is the finding that 62.8 percent of the sample was intemperate. McCook assumed, as a matter of course, that destitution followed from drunkenness, not vice versa. However, the question ("20. Temperate, intemperate, or abstainer?") was sufficiently vague that causality could not be inferred from tabulated replies alone. More generally, the language and method of this survey, and others that followed,[2] reflected his initial tendency to look for personal weaknesses in the poor rather than structural problems such as unemployment (McCook, 1893b; Green, 1979). Compounding this problem was the fact that McCook began his statistical investigations relatively early, before the great flood of social surveys (Eaton and Harrison, 1930) and the revolution in inferential statistics in the early twentieth century. With few advanced survey models and virtually no understanding of probability or correlation, he was restricted to compiling and comparing averages drawn from uneven, hit-or-miss samples. That was hardly his fault—he was, after all, merely following the prevailing statistical practices—but it does inevitably diminish the value of his work for modern researchers.

Fortunately, however, McCook supplemented his survey efforts with extensive interviews. Large numbers of vagrants passed through Hartford, a major railway junction, and McCook took the opportunity to question them. Cordial and noncondescending, his inquiries yielded information on a range of topics, including drinking practices, vote selling, and begging techniques (French, 1977:31; SRP: Series III, Rolls4–6; cf. Boyer, 1978:202–204).

As he became more familiar with their world, McCook developed a certain empathy, even guarded fondness, for these disheveled wanderers. With one, William "Roving Bill" Aspinwall, he carried on a twenty-five-year correspondence. Aspinwall, a Union veteran and onetime correspondent of a rural newspaper, sent McCook long, picaresque accounts of life among the *"Haut Beaus."* Although his letters testify to the devastating effects of the 1893 depression, Aspinwall also admitted that he "would be a well to do man today" if it had not been for lapses into intemperance, reinforcing McCook's conviction that drinking was a major source of the tramp problem (SRP: Roll 12, Frame 871; J. McCook,

1901–1902).

But drinking what? One popular belief held that the real source of the problem was adulterated and inferior spirits:

I had heard much of the powers of "lightning" whiskey, "tanglefoot," and "kill me quick," and of the benignity of "private stock," and other club brands of mellifluous name and high price. Of the whiskey sold in one part of the town, I had heard it asserted, half in earnest, that you could "engrave on glass with it." No wonder, therefore, that the poor fellows cheated into buying it were made crazy and criminals. The pure whiskey sold in the other part of town could, on the contrary, be consumed without other results than a gentle booze, followed, possibly, by a mild headache.
Was all this true? (McCook, 1894:8).

To find out, McCook gathered and chemically analyzed whiskey specimens from all over the city. To his surprise, he discovered that the cheapest brands were probably the least harmful, since they were among the most diluted ("You know water don't hurt nobody" was the way Hartford publicans tactfully put it). McCook concluded that "it is not the adulteration of whiskey which does the business, but the amount of alcohol taken, and the rapidity with which it is taken." He observed that vagrants who had cadged a small stake would retire to their favorite saloons, there to down anywhere from fifteen to twenty-five drinks during a twelve-hour period. Although they were drinking a watered product, the sheer volume of intake insured that they were consuming large amounts of alcohol, usually on an empty stomach. Many tramps (including Aspinwall) stayed away from whiskey, preferring beer or ale because they contained more alcohol for the money. But the beer alcoholics were no less thirsty for their economy; they would drink from twenty to forty nickel glasses during a noon-to-midnight binge (J. McCook, 1894:11–12 and 1901–1902:24).

When it came to describing such prodigalities, McCook did not rely entirely upon words and statistics. Between 1893 and 1895 he arranged for three series of photographs to be taken. The first consisted of individual and group portraits of tramps, who were paid a quarter apiece to visit the studio of Hartford photographer Charles T. Stuart.[3] "A Common Shovel Bum" is a good example of this type—full length, no backdrop, no props, the pose left to the individual. There is about these tramps a quiet dignity; knowing they were going to be photographed, they made the best of their appearance, however ragged or weary or intoxicated they may have been. McCook was pleased with these portraits but recognized the limitations of studio work. Trying to capture his subjects in a more natural environment, McCook engaged professional photographers to accompany him to saloons, police stations, and lodging houses in New York City, Boston, and

"*A Common Shovel Bum.. Father...a saloon keeper & drinking man; mother all right...has tramped off and on for 15 years..Property man in Buffalo Bill's show and in Theatrical Co....'Yes, of course you know I drink. Lost my place in Buf. Bill's by getting on a boose'...*" *(SRP: Roll 4, Frames 312–313; Roll 11, Frames 1062–1063.)*

Butler-McCook Homestead Collection, courtesy The Antiquarian and Landmarks Society, Inc., Hartford, CT.

Hartford, there to take "interior flash light views" (SRP: Roll 11, Frame 827).
Judging from their appearance, these photographs were mostly unposed. The
technique resembles some of Jacob Riis's early forays into the underworld: set up
the camera, ignite a magnesium cartridge, gather up the equipment, and head for the
next location (Alland, 1974:26–27). Two of the New York City photographs,
"Bum Beer Saloon" and "Just a Common Drunk," are included here. Taken
together, they graphically illustrate the cause and effect of the drink problem, at
least as McCook then understood it. The same may be said of "The Feast:
Liquids." This was part of a third series of photographs taken by McCook's son,
Philip, in the Hartford area in 1895. These were mainly posed, outdoor shots,
designed to illustrate some aspect of tramp life, such as train jumping or bibulous
picnics.

*"Bum Beer Saloon, N.Y. Five cents for anything. Down town. East Side. Feb. 22. A.D. 1895. About 11:30 P.M."
[Clock actually shows 10:20 p.m.] This was "the Bill Goat," 153 Park Row. A police detective, J. J. Murphy, wrote to
McCook that "they serve a free lunch there consisting of Beef Stew and Soup, on Friday they give Fish Chowder, the
proprietor is a Russian Jew named Bernard Kommel." Judging from his attire and prominent place, Kommel is the
mustachioed gentleman in the left foreground. He later wrote McCook reminding him to send a promised copy of the
photograph; evidently he was proud of his establishment, the strictures of Orthodox Judaism and the morality of
inquiring Protestants notwithstanding (SRP: Roll 11, Frames 891, 904, 1182).*

"'Just a Common Drunk.' 4th Precinct Stationhouse, Oak St. N.Y. Feb 22. A.D. 1895. 11:15 P.M." *The sergeant on duty explained that the police patrol would be augmented after midnight, "because saloons close and send their contents out to commit disorder" (SRP: Roll 4, Frame 954; Roll 11, Frame 1180).*

"The Feast. Liquids. The dyke. May 5. A.D. 1895. *"The dyke was on the southeastern outskirts of Hartford, bordering the Connecticut River; nearby was the large bull barn where tramps slept in the hay. While waiting for their stew to cook a man named Murphy entertained the group by singing ballads: "Though they laugh at funny things they above all dote on the triumph of virtue and the bad end of the villain, and love to have their hearts wrung by the picture of human grief" (SRP:: Roll 4, Frames 1028–1035; Roll 11, Frame 1239).*

What was McCook trying to accomplish with these photographs? He was certainly not an impassioned photojournalist, seeking to shock the public out of its complacency—although a few of his lodging house views have a power that rivals the work of Riis. McCook's attitude toward photographs seems relatively cautious and neutral; he would use them for illustrative purposes in his lectures and articles, but at the same time denied that they adequately depicted all the forces operating on their subjects (SRP: Roll 1, Frames 954–976, 1070; J. McCook, 1901–1902:3010). For McCook the photographic image was necessarily subordinate to statistics and other, more rigorous categories of evidence. Yet, to paraphrase Wright Morris, the secret ingredient in photographs is time. Today McCook's photographs appear to be the most striking and valuable part of his legacy, while his painstakingly compiled questionnaires seem flawed and dated.

Perhaps that is too quick a judgment. There is another way to look at McCook's photographs and statistics, quite aside from their relative fidelity to the facts of lower-class life. Like his chemical analyses and detailed interviews, they are symptomatic of a larger change in the discourse of reform. Earlier in the nineteenth century, emphasis was placed on overt moral appeals, with temperance lecturers using dramatic, personal stories to sway their audiences; but by 1900 there was a growing reliance on statistics, sociological investigation, and "objective" analysis, "a strategy characteristic of many otherwise quite disparate Progressive reforms" (Boyer, 1978:198–202; quotation at 198). McCook's investigations, though flawed, were a harbinger, an early demonstration of the aggregative and objectifying impulses that would soon dominate alcohol studies, indeed dominate the investigation of virtually all twentieth-century social problems.

McCook's Developing Thought on Alcohol and Alcoholism

Once McCook's career as a social reformer was launched in the 1890s, he branched out in several directions. In addition to the projects already mentioned, he published exposés of political corruption, especially the buying of votes with cash or liquor; planned and lobbied (unsuccessfully) for a Connecticut state reformatory; and gathered information on the prevalence and treatment of venereal disease.[4] Regardless of which social concern he took up, drink always seemed to be a factor; it was the one thread running through all his investigations.[5] In one 1895 lecture he charged that drinking was responsible, in varying degrees, for abused and abandoned children, homicide, vagabondage, pauperism, insanity, contagion, licentiousness, and venal voting (J. McCook, 1895a:2–4).

Although he was initially convinced that drink was the *fons et origo* of social problems, and never entirely abandoned this belief, McCook did subsequently modify his views, in response to new evidence and changing social and medical theories of alcoholism. With respect to tramps, for example, McCook noticed that their ranks swelled with the onset of financial panics or depressions. In 1873 and again in 1893 there were large increases in the number of itinerant poor in Massachusetts and presumably elsewhere. Confronted with this data, McCook abandoned his original, simple model (intemperance spawns tramps) for one that emphasized the interaction between drinking and the economy. When depression hit, payrolls had to be cut, and drinking men—the least efficient workers—were the first to go. Single men went next, married men last of all. Since "the tramp is generally a drunkard self-confessed; and an unmarried man by his own admission" he was doubly at risk for unemployment; he might hold down a job for awhile, but hard times would almost invariably find him out of work and on the road (J. McCook, 1895b:168–170; McCook and Johnson, 1922:413; Ringenbach, 1973:xiv–xv, 60, 62; Bruns, 1977:144). This did not entirely absolve the tramp—he was, for McCook, still a drunkard—but it did make his situation morally more complex. The business cycle was certainly not within his, or anyone's, control.[6]

McCook's views on alcoholism itself also became more nuanced and less judgmental. In the 1891 outdoor alms report alcoholism figured as an aggravating and expensive vice, a product of individual weakness. By 1901, however, McCook was speaking publicly of environmental influences. He pointed out that homeless children, neglected and abused by drunken parents, often became alcoholics before they reached their majority (J. McCook, 1901:12). Unless something happened to break the chain, their children would grow up in similarly wretched circumstances, with similar results.

McCook was somewhat influenced by the inebriety movement, which held that alcoholism and drug addiction were functional diseases, triggered by an underlying mental disturbance. According to this theory, which won growing numbers of adherents in the late nineteenth century, individuals who inherited or acquired an abnormal or weakened nervous system stood an especially good chance of becoming inebriates. Drink enslaved them; it further damaged their nervous constitutions; and it increased the likelihood that their children would inherit a tendency toward inebriety. The condition was not necessarily irreversible; isolation, rest, and retraining, if intelligently and humanely planned, might effect a cure. By coincidence, the leading American apostle of the inebriety movement, Thomas Davison Crothers, was a Hartford resident and political ally of McCook's (SRP: Roll 14, Frame 945; see also Jaffe, 1978).

Elements of the inebriety approach appear in McCook's writings as early as 1895. He observed, for example, that "to deal with drunkards and drunken men requires expert knowledge. For drunkenness is in reality insanity; and insanity requires for its handling much science and some unusual gifts" (J. McCook, 1895a:5). Elsewhere he wrote of the desirability of segregating tramps in a reformatory "for a year or more, which allows nature to throw off the alcoholic degeneration of nerve tissue...." (J. McCook, 1895b:180). But McCook never developed a firm commitment to this or any other medical model of addiction. Part of the problem was the inebriety theorists' fundamental assertion that drunkenness was not sinful, that it had to be understood strictly in terms of nervous disease. One writer, Charles Follen Palmer, went so far as to label ridiculous the "fallacy that criminality or viciousness is a moral infraction, a voluntary transgression rather than a mental deformity" (Palmer, 1898:102; cf. Jellinek, 1968:207–210). From this type of determinism, Reverend McCook drew back—halfway. In one memorable passage in a 1901 sermon he referred to alcoholism variously as insanity, sin, and a social and economic problem (J. McCook,.1901:13). Whether these conflicting views reflect a subtle sociological imagination, able to comprehend a problem from several different perspectives or merely a divided mind, floundering among rapidly shifting intellectual currents, is difficult to say. Another possibility is that McCook's ideas on the nature of alcoholism were tentative and fragmentary simply because he never gave the etiological question much sustained thought. Instead, he concentrated his energies on the *effects* of alcoholism, which he took to be the really pressing concern. This was true, not only of McCook, but of most late nineteenth and early twentieth-century reformers; they were much more preoccupied with the social and economic costs of drinking than the moral or medical condition of the individual alcoholic (Levine, 1978:161).

Solutions

McCook did part company with other Progessive reformers, however, on the issue of prohibition. In 1891 he wrote that

> I have the greatest sympathy with prohibitionists. They are deeply in earnest, and they are, in one point, far ahead of the average of us—they have some adequate sense of the importance of the drink question. But I cannot but feel that their way never can, and possibly never ought to, be given them. I say "possibly" with deliberation. If all else failed, and it came to be a question finally of whether I should have to part with my liberty to the drunkard or he part with his to me,...I should take his freedom away....But until that possibility becomes actual fact I do not favor prohibition—as a political issue least of all (J. McCook, 1893a:106).

McCook's reluctance to endorse prohibition was due, in part, to his personal and liturgical use of alcohol, in part to his conviction that such laws were largely unenforceable and that bootlegging was a poor substitute for the open saloon.[7] His doubts about prohibition did not, however, lead to quietism on the liquor issue. He developed an alternative program, in some respects more draconian than prohibition itself.

The first point was prevention. Convinced that "it is the alcohol that does the business," McCook argued that the essential thing was to restrict the amount consumed by an individual drinker (J. McCook, 1895a:14). The problem was that saloonkeepers and liquor dealers had no incentive to do so, since their profits were proportional to the number of drinks or bottles sold. But if private sellers could be taken out of the picture, and control vested in fixed-profit municipal monopolies, as in Sweden and Norway, then liquor could be sold "legally and rationally, refusing minors, paupers, and drunkards, and selling only in moderation to any." Such an arrangement would raise revenue, save money by reducing the number of dependent drunkards, and alleviate corruption, because "temperate men...are found to be for the most part non-purchasable" (J. McCook, 1892c:175–176; cf. Lender and Martin, 1982:104–106).

But what of those who were already alcoholics? McCook's answer was blunt: "shut up drunkards of every condition, whether violent or not." Not, however, in jails; they needed to be confined in specially designed institutions where they would work, learn trades, and other "useful habits." Sentencing would be indeterminate and "regulated by a wise system of parole" (J. McCook, 1893a). McCook also urged that drunkards and vagabonds, in reformatories or out, be disfranchised (SRP: Roll 7, Frames 428–430; J. McCook, 1892c: 173–174). Even though they had not committed a felony, their chronic troublemaking and proclivity for vote selling justified their exclusion from the electorate.[8]

Roger Bruns, an authority on tramps and hoboes, has labeled McCook's program one of repression (Bruns, 1980:72). That it was, but it is worth considering the mixture of motives behind it. McCook wanted to force alcoholics back into the mainstream of society, to discipline them out of their expensive folly/disease. But this was not merely because they were a threat. He also sought to help them as human beings, or, in the favored expression of the day, to uplift them, to save their bodies from paupers' graves and their souls from damnation. If he were only interested in naked control he would have settled for incarceration; however, he spent years planning and fighting for a Connecticut reformatory, where alcoholics and vagrants could be isolated from hardened criminals and intelligently rehabilitated (see note 4). In this McCook was, again, stereotypically Progressive. As Paul Boyer has shown, many of McCook's contemporaries, such as Jacob Riis and Theodore Roosevelt, combined coercive and environmental approaches to social problems. "It is a dreary old truth," Riis noted, "that those who would fight *for* the poor must *fight* the poor to do it." When Progressives looked at the new urban-industrial landscape, they saw it with a kind of double vision: it was at once a menace to be subdued and a moral habitat to be ameliorated (Boyer, 1978:175–187, 190; quotation at 176). Stated another way, Progressives like McCook saw no irreconcilable conflict between social justice and social control; indeed, they "set about methodically to achieve justice through control" (Link and McCormick, 1983:70; see also Grob, 1979:149, 151–152).

Not that McCook was insensitive to questions of individual freedom. "I like liberty and believe in it," he once wrote, without a trace of disingenuousness (J. McCook, 1895a:9). He knew that the sort of remedies he advocated curtailed accustomed freedoms, and thus required careful justification. Here he fell back upon a detailed analysis of social costs. The community had a moral right to control alcoholics or regulate liquor dealers because their activities resulted in palpable economic harm—so many extra dollars for alms, asylums, police, and so forth. He drew an analogy to the confiscation of cholera-contaminated watermelons: "Individual liberty to sell or eat simply vanishes before the liberty of the community to escape death and expense" (J. McCook, 1895a:1; see also SRP: Roll 1, Frames 77–78). Alcohol obviously did not pose a threat as immediate and terrifying as cholera, but since it sapped the community through numerous and burdensome expenses, its control was also justified.

McCook as a Transitional Figure

All of this has a very contemporary ring; in recent years it has become commonplace to justify coercive measures, especially those involving noninfectious diseases, on the basis of social costs. This style of argumentation, which has been variously described as the new paternalism, neocameralism, and the new public health (Bonnie, 1978; Courtwright, 1980; Watts, 1982), was natural to McCook; indeed, were he still alive, he would be greatly amused at its presumed novelty.

It will not do to set up McCook as a prophet, however, for there were about him vestiges of the past as well as inklings of the future. "The 'new public health' approach," Thomas Watts has recently written, "does not state that alcohol (or alcoholism) is sinful or bad (unlike the Prohibition era), nor does it state that the alcoholic is necessarily set apart and 'sick' (disease conception of alcoholism), but it does state that increased alcohol consumption in a society does connect with increased societal health problems, that social control over alcohol must be a prime societal, policy concern" (Watts, 1982:1238). Yet the fascinating thing about McCook is that his work reflects all three of these traditions. Because of his upbringing, he felt that alcoholics were unworthy; because of his exposure to the inebriety movement, he sometimes described them as diseased; and because of his concern with civic economy, he learned to think systematically about alcohol and its control. McCook's career is significant not because of his impact on policy—his recommendations were largely ignored[9] by a generation bent on a root-and-branch solution—but because it is so microcosmic. It sets off, against the background of progressivism, virtually every important strand of social thought on alcoholism during the last hundred years.

NOTES

1. For a partial but representative list of McCook's reference materials, see SRP: Series IV, Roll 6. McCook's travels in Europe and elsewhere were often for reasons of health. A classic "workaholic," he repeatedly pushed himself to the brink of endurance—and sometimes beyond it. Then he would take a vacation. But even while traveling he was constantly observing and writing, e.g., SRP: Roll 5, Notebook LXXIII. Most of the foregoing details on McCook's early life and career are taken from the biographical and autobiographical fragments in SRP: Roll 7, Appendices A and B, and the Scotch-Irish Society of America, n.d.

2. In 1892 McCook conducted a second survey, "Chiefs of Police re Tramps and Drunkenness," the title of which is self-explanatory. In 1893–1894 he sent yet another questionnaire, "Drink and Pauperism," to Connecticut selectmen, attempting to ascertain what percentage of their relief expenditures were traceable to drink. The replies, correspondence, and miscellaneous survey material are in SRP: Roll 3. The "Casual Lodgers or Tramps" results are in SRP: Roll 2.

3. Occasionally tramps were photographed elsewhere, but Stuart did the vast majority of the studio work. McCook also filled out questionnaires on each of the subjects and often interviewed them at length, jotting comments in his notebooks or on the backs of photographs. Some of these comments appear in the captions below the photographs.

4. On venal voting, see SRP: Series X, Roll 10, and J. McCook, 1892b and 1892c. Material on syphilis is in SRP: Series IV, Roll 6; Series VIII, Roll 9, Folder L and Roll 11, Folder B; see also J. McCook, 1892a:355–360. The state reformatory controversy is documented in SRP: Series XIII, Rolls 13 and 14. At first the legislature backed McCook's reformatory plans, but withdrew its support in 1897 due to cost concerns. The plan was also vigorously opposed by a group of Hartford property owners who did not want a reformatory situated nearby. McCook replied with carefully prepared arguments, emphasizing the long-term benefits of such a facility. He lost anyway. Like other statistically minded reformers, McCook believed that "quantitative research, when merged with administrative rationality, could replace politics;" when it did not, he was bitterly disappointed (Grob, 1978:quotation at 139; French, 1977:23).

5. For all the emphasis on alcohol, it is interesting that McCook paid virtually no attention to other drugs. There are two reasons for this. First, drug (especially opiate) addicts were largely concentrated in the upper and middle classes at the turn of the century (Courtwright, 1982). They were thus not much in evidence in almshouses or other charitable institutions. For example, in the John James McCook Papers, Watkinson Library, Trinity College, Hartford, there is a list of Hartford almshouse residents for 1894. Although roughly two-thirds were classified as drunkards, only three of 536, or 0.56 percent, were listed as opium users. A second consideration is that narcotics users were relatively tranquil and sedated, while drinkers comported themselves more aggressively. "The man drunk with opium reclines upon his couch, and resigns himself to the contemplation of his

visions," observed the Reverend J. Townley Crane, "...the man drugged with alcohol usually becomes a miserable compound of brute and devil" (Crane, 1858:565). This, of course, is a generalization, but it does help to explain why alcoholics were perceived as a more serious and immediate social threat.

6.   McCook also scaled down his estimates of the amount of poverty traceable to alcohol.   In *The Drink Business* he stated that 62.8 percent of vagabonds and 71 percent of paupers were intemperate, and "the conclusion seems a fair one that drink had something to do with" their impoverished condition (J. McCook, 1895a:2–3). However, when the Committee of Fifty for the Investigation of the Liquor Problem, of which McCook was a member, discussed a preliminary summary of its work in early 1904, McCook accepted the finding that "about 25 percent[of poverty] can be traced directly or indirectly to liquor." He quibbled with some details in the draft, but the passage on poverty bears no critical annotations on McCook's copy, and he elsewhere expressed general satisfaction with its conclusions (SRP: Roll 9, Folder H, especially Frames 1283, 1289; Koren, 1899:21).

7.   This was also the position of the Committee of Fifty, mentioned in the note above (Wines and Koren, 1897:5).   However, when national prohibition was enacted McCook grudgingly accepted it, on the grounds that it initially had a popular mandate and that "the immediate and inescapable obligation of everybody is absolute Obedience to the Existing Law" (SRP: Roll 9, Frames 1300–1301).

8.   It is worth noting, however, that McCook condemned the Southern Style of disfranchisement as a thinly disguised form of racial discrimination.   He believed that the only legitimate criteria for evaluating prospective voters were education and responsibility, and that these standards had to be applied uniformly to all groups (McCook, 1912:178–179). Control, in other words, was to be tempered by justice.

9.   Ironically, McCook's ideas were a virtual blueprint of what would happen with narcotics in the United States.   During 1915–1930 narcotics were subject to progressively tighter regulations, designed to limit their use to medical practice; nonmedical addicts became, for all intents and purposes, felons, and were thus generally unable to vote; and specialized institutions (e.g., the Lexington and Fort Worth Hospitals) were created to house and rehabilitate addicts (Musto, 1973; Courtwright, 1982).

REFERENCES

Aaron, Paul, and David Musto
    1981   Temperance and Prohibition in America: A Historical Overview.   In
        Alcohol and Public Policy, edited by Mark H. Moore and Dean R. Gerstein,
        127–181. Washington, D.C.: National Academy Press.
Alland, Alexander, Sr.
    1974   *Jacob A. Riis: Photographer & Citizen*. Millerton, N.Y.: Aperture, Inc.
Bonnie, Richard J.
    1978   Discouraging Unhealthy Personal Choices: Reflections on New Directions
        in Substance Abuse Policy. *Journal of Drug issues* 8:199–219.
Boyer, Paul C.

1978   *Urban Masses and Moral Order in America, 1820-1920.*   Cambridge, Mass.: Harvard University Press.

Bremner, Robert H.
1980   *The Public Good: Philanthropy and Welfare in the Civil War Era.*   New York: Alfred A. Knopf.

Bruns, Roger
1977   Hoboes Told All to 1890s Scholar. *Smithsonian* 8, no. 8:141–151.
1980   *Knights of the Road: A Hobo History.* New York: Methuen.

Courtwright, David T.
1980   Public Health and Public Wealth: Social Costs as a Basis for Restrictive Policies.   *Millbank Memorial Fund Quarterly: Health and Society* 58:268–281.
1982   *Dark Paradise: Opiate Addiction in America before 1940.*   Cambridge, Mass.:   Harvard University Press.

Crane, J. Townley
1858   Drugs as an Indulgence. *Methodist Quarterly Review* 40:551–566.

Eaton, Allen, in collaboration with Shelby M. Harrison
1930   *A Bibliography of Social Surveys: Reports of Fact-finding Studies Made as a Basis For Social Action; Arranged by Subjects and Localities; Reports to January 1, 1928.* New York: Russell Sage Foundation.

French, Adela Haberski
1977   *The Social Reform Papers of John James McCook: A Guide to the Microfilm Collection.*   Hartford: The Antiquarian and Landmarks Society, Inc.

Green, Howard
1979   'A Devil of a lot of questions':   Reverend John McCook and His 1891 Tramp Survey.   Unpublished paper read at the annual meeting of the Organization of American Historians.

Grob, Gerald N.
1978   *Edward Jarvis and the Medical World of Nineteenth-Century America.* Knoxville: University of Tennessee Press.
1979   Rediscovering Asylums: The Unhistorical History of the Mental Hospital.   In *The Therapeutic Revolution,* edited by Morris Vogel and Charles E. Rosenberg, 133–157.   Philadelphia: University of Pennsylvania Press.

Jaffe, A.
1978   Reform in American Medical Science: The Inebriety Movement and the Origins of the Psychological Disease Theory of Addiction, 1870–1920. *British Journal of Addiction* 73:139–147.

Jellinek, E. M.
1968   *The Disease Concept of Alcoholism.*   New Haven and New Brunswick, N.J.:   College and University Press in association with Hillhouse Press, fourth printing.

Koren, John
  1899   *Economic Aspects of the Liquor Problem: An Investigation Made for the Committee of Fifty under the Direction of Henry W. Farnam, Secretary of the Economic Sub-Committee.* Boston and New York: Houghton Mifflin Co.
Lender, Mark Edward, and James Kirby Martin
  1982   *Drinking in America: A History.* New York and London: The Free Press and Collier Macmillan.
Levine, Harry Gene
  1978   The Discovery of Addiction: Changing Conceptions of Habitual Drunkenness in America. *Journal of Studies on Alcohol* 39:143–174.
Link, Arthur S., and Richard L. McCormick
  1983   *Progressivism.* Arlington Heights, Ill.: Harlan Davidson.
[McCook, John J.]
  1891   *Report of the Special Committee on Outdoor Alms of the Town of Hartford A. D. 1891.* Hartford: Case, Lockwood & Brainard.
McCook, John J.
  1892a   Some New Phases of the Tramp Problem. *The Charities Review* 1:355–364.
  1892b   The Alarming Proportion of Venal Voters. *The Forum* 14:1–13.
  1892c   Venal Voting: Methods and Remedies. *The Forum* 14:159–177.
  1893a   Practical Politics: What Can Clergymen Do About It? *The Homiletic Review* 25:483–490; 26:99–108.
  1893b   A Tramp Census and Its Revelations. *The Forum* 15:753–766.
  1894   Pauperism and Whiskey. Reprint from the *Journal of Social Science* for November, 1894.
  1895a   *The Drink Business. What it is; what it does; what to do with it. A Business Talk.* Hartford: Twentieth Century Club.
  1895b   The Tramp Problem. *Lend a Hand* 15:167–183.
  1901   *Dreams and Visions: A Sermon Preached at the Opening of the Convention of the Diocese of Connecticut in Trinity Church, New Haven, St. Barnabas' Day, June 11 A.D. 1901.* New Haven: Tuttle, Morehouse & Taylor.
  1901–   Leaves from the Diary of a Tramp. *The Independent* 53:2760–2767,
  1902   2880–2888, 3009–3013, 54:23–28, 154–160, 332–337, 620–624, 873–874, 1539–1544.
  1912   *War—The Soldier's Testimony Regarding It. Sermon Before the Commandery of the State of New York of the Military Order of the Loyal Legion of the United States, at their Annual Church Service, April 10, 1910, in the Church of the Incarnation, New York.* New York: The Knickerbocker Press.
  1977   *The Social Reform Papers of John James McCook* (SRP). Fourteen microfilm rolls. Hartford: The Antiquarian and Landmarks Society of Connecticut.
  n.d.   John James McCook Papers. The Watkinson Library, Trinity College, Hartford, Conn.

McCook, John James, and Alvin Saunders Johnson
   1922   Tramp. *New International Encyclopedia*   22:413–414.   New York: Dodd,
          Mead and Co.
McCook, Philip James
   1964   *The Days of My Age.* Privately printed.
Musto, David F.
   1973   *The American Disease: Origins of Narcotic Control.*   New Haven: Yale
          University Press.
Palmer, Charles Follen
   1898   *Inebriety: Its Source, Prevention, and Cure.*   New York: Fleming H.
          Revell.
Ringenbach, Paul T.
   1973   *Tramps and Reformers, 1873–1916:   The Discovery of Unemployment in
          New York.* Westport, Conn.: Greenwood Press.
Scotch-Irish Society of America
   n.d.   *A Brief Historical Sketch of the "Fighting McCooks."*   New York: James
          Kempster Printing Company.
Timberlake, James H.
   1966   *Prohibition and the Progressive Movement.*   Cambridge, Mass.:   Harvard
          University Press.
Watts, Thomas D.
   1982   Three Traditions in Social Thought on Alcoholism.   *International Journal
          of the Addictions* 17:1231–1239.
Wiebe, Robert H.
   1977   *The Search for Order, 1877–1920.* New York: Hill and Wang.
Wines, Frederic H., and John Koren
   1897   *The Liquor Problem in Its Legislative Aspects: An Investigation Made
          Under the Direction of Charles W. Eliot, Seth Low and James C. Carter, Sub-
          Committee of the Committee of Fifty to Investigate the Liquor Problem.*
          Boston and New York: Houghton Mifflin Co.

CURRENT SOCIAL THOUGHT ON ALCOHOL AND MARIJUANA: A QUANTITATIVE EXPLORATION

Barbara Lynn Kail

Social thought on alcohol and drugs has undergone a process of medicalization in recent years. Now we see the possible emergence of a public health model, characterized by renewed concern with the substance alcohol and a systemic or ecological view of the user. Through a secondary analysis of data collected by L. Harris and Associates in 1974 for the National Institute on Alcoholism and Alcohol Abuse, this paper attempts to address the following questions: Is such a model present in current thought on marijuana, or is this substance in the process of being medicalized? How closely linked is the public's perception of these two drugs?

Problem and Background

Are we witnessing a revolution in social thought on alcohol and marijuana? Our thinking about these two substances is currently in a state of flux. The prevailing model or paradigm may be shifting from a medical to a systemic orientation. Kuhn (1970) describes such transitions from one conceptual framework to another as revolutions, generated by the persistent failure of the old framework to make sense of anomalous findings. To this author's knowledge, there have not been any recent studies of public opinion attempting to document changes in social thought on alcohol and marijuana.

This shift in thought would not be the first. A number of authors have described the transition from a moral or religious orientation to the currently held medical perspective. The former paradigm was characterized by a deep concern about, respect for, and dislike of the substance alcohol. Even moderate use of this powerful drug was believed to cause addiction. The user of alcohol was perceived as a morally weak individual succumbing to the pleasures of this drug (Conrad and Schneider, 1980; Levine, 1978; Watts, 1982). Since the 1940s, a medical paradigm has gained widespread support, characterized by relatively little concern about the substance and increased concern about the abuser. Jellinek presents in codified form the tenets of this model: alcoholics have identifiable predisposing characteristics; alcoholism is a progressive, inexorable process; alcoholics lose control when drinking; abstinence is the only means of treatment (Conrad and Schneider, 1980). Available opinion polls report that from 50 to 66 percent of the

Barbara Kail is currently an associate professor at The University of Texas at Arlington, Graduate School of Social Work. She received a D.S.W. from the Columbia University School of Social Work in 1981. She has been involved in research on drug abuse since 1974; currently she is conducting a study of decision making and prescription drug use by the elderly. Her other interest in this area is substance abuse by women.

samples studied defined alcoholism as an illness (Haberman and Scheinberg, 1969; Linsky, 1970; Mulford and Miller, 1964; Reiss, 1977).

The disease model is currently being challenged by a public health model based upon general systems theory. This paradigm is characterized by a renewed belief that alcohol is a problematic substance, and that the heavy user of alcohol is no different from others (Beauchamp, 1980). Recent studies have questioned the need for alcoholics to abstain from alcohol, generating heated debate (Brody, 1976; 1980a; 1980b). Difficulties in identifying predisposing characteristics of alcoholics and a focus on "problem drinking" as opposed to alcoholism are yet two more challenges (Cahalan, 1970; Cahalan et al., 1969; Cahalan and Room, 1974). Finally, mounting concern about the effect alcohol consumption has on our industries and highways indicates an increasingly systemic perspective of the user.

Opinion on marijuana may be in even greater flux. It certainly seems to have changed more rapidly over a shorter period of time. Current policy continues to be based on a moral model dating from the Marijuana Tax Act of 1937. Yet, the winds are shifting rapidly. The meteoric increase in marijuana use during the 1960s probably both expressed and caused a changing perception of the drug (National Commission, 1972). Actions of interest groups such as NORML and the decriminalization of marijuana possession in a number of states are political expressions of such a change. It is not clear, however, which direction this change will take. Thought may be shifting to a medical model. The decreasing concern with marijuana as a dangerous substance and an increasing concern with the abuser are indications of a change in this direction. A further example is Reagan's increasing commitment to the treatment of "soft" drug users (ADAMHA, 1981). On the other hand, the mass media continue to express an increasing awareness of the impact marijuana may have on the larger society—particularly on our highways and in the military. Continuing debates about the physical consequences of marijuana use suggest we retain a strong concern about the substance (National Institute on Drug Abuse, 1980). Furthermore, one study based on data from the NORC General Social Survey does report that only 29 percent of the sample favored legalization of marijuana (Singh et al., 1979). The issues and findings just discussed all point to a systems-oriented, public health paradigm.

The changing views on alcohol and marijuana discussed above do not rest on empirically validated measures of public opinion, however. Most available material is qualitative in nature. The available quantitative studies are often based on samples of dubious representativeness (for an excellent review of studies on opinion toward marijuana see Singh et al., 1979).

In response to the question initially proposed, this study attempts to delineate:

- Current views on the substances alcohol and marijuana.
- Current views on the users of these substances.

- How respondent characteristics are related to the views they hold.
- How perceptions of alcohol and marijuana are related.
- The extent to which these perceptions support a public health or systems-oriented model.

Methodology

This study is a secondary analysis of data collected by L. Harris in January of 1974. A random multi-stage cluster sampling design was used to obtain a sample representative of the U.S. population eighteen years and older (N=1,594). Gender and age distributions are similar to census distributions. Blacks may be underrepresented (Martin et al., 1981). Respondents in this study are largely white (88 percent) and married (84 percent). The size and representativeness of this sample outweigh the disadvantages caused by the age of these data; there is no existing data set containing the measures of interest here that is more current.

Trained staff conducted face-to-face interviews with respondents in their homes.

For both alcohol and marijuana, measures were developed from the available data to assess perception of the substance, perception of the user, and policy recommendations. Figure 1 describes these measures and presents the Cronbach Alpha, mean, and range for each scale.

Some of these concepts are more successfully measured than others. The scale measuring policy recommendations for alcohol is weak. It covers only the individual treatment aspect and is lacking in reliability. The two questions assessing perception of the marijuana user lack reliability when added to form a scale and do not measure the concept as directly as possible. Caution will be used when interpreting findings based on these measures.

Findings

What is current public opinion on alcohol and marijuana? The average person in this sample perceives alcohol to be a problematic substance (X=6.35) and does not see the alcoholic as different from other people (X=7.65). Treatment of problem drinkers is still heavily influenced by the medical model (X=6.33). Marijuana use in this country is also believed to be a serious problem (X=3.37). Yet, public opinion of the users of this substance remains in flux. The mean for this scale, 3.61, is almost midway between the two poles of perceiving the user as engaging in aberrant behavior which he/she will grow out of, contrasted with behavior that is as acceptable as the occasional recreational use of alcohol. There is a clear consensus against legalization of marijuana (X=3.93) (see Figure 1).

What are the characteristics of those most likely to view alcohol as a problematic substance, one of the crucial distinctions between a medical and systems-oriented paradigm? Older (r=.07), religiously active (r=.11) Protestants (r=.05) are most likely to see alcohol use as a serious problem. Male (r=-.11)

FIGURE 1: For Alcohol and Marijuana: Measures of Attitude Toward the Substance, the User and Policy

Measure	Description	Cronbach Alpha	Mean	Range
Perception of alcohol as a problematic substance	Respondents were asked if heavy drinking of alcoholic beverages and drunken driving were problems. Responses were summed into a Likert scale.	.57	6.35	2–7
Perception of the alcoholic as different	Respondents were asked the extent to which the following statements were basically true, partially true, or mostly false: No one turns into an alcoholic unless he is unhappy to begin with; it takes years of heavy drinking before becoming an alcoholic; no one with a good moral or religious background becomes an alcoholic; if people drink too much, it's because they are under pressure; a person is an alcoholic only if he gives up eating regularly and taking care of his health.	.67	7.65	5–15
Treatment of alcoholics	Statements concerning the appropriateness of jailing, hospitalizing, and helping employees who drink were summed into a Likert scale.	.43	6.33	3–8
Perception of marijuana as a problematic substance	One question asking respondents whether marijuana use was a very serious, moderately serious, or not too serious a problem, or not a problem at all.		3.37	1–4
Future use of marijuana as a recreational drug	Respondents were asked whether they believed marijuana would be used like alcohol in the future and whether the younger generation will continue to use marijuana in the future. These yes/no responses were summed into a Likert scale.	.43	3.61	2–6
Legalization of marijuana	These questions were summed into a Likert Scale—whether the use or sale of marijuana should be legalized and whether possession of marijuana should be illegal but punished only by a small fine.	.83	3.93	3–6

educated (r=-.06) Democrats (r=-.05) who did not vote in 1972 (r=-.05) are least likely to hold this view. A multiple regression indicates that of these predictors, sex and religious activity are most important (see Table 1).

How related are perceptions of marijuana and alcohol? Those who perceive alcohol to be a serious problem tend to see the alcoholic as no different from others (r=-.10), believe marijuana use is also a serious problem (r=.31), and oppose the legalization of marijuana (r=-.13). Despite the impact of the demographic variables described above, perception of the alcoholic and of marijuana use as serious problems are the strongest predictors of perception of alcohol as a problematic substance (see Table 1).

Together, the predictors considered here account for 13 percent of the variation in perception of alcohol as a problematic substance.

These findings are all significant but weak.

Table 1:   Multiple Regression of Selected Demographic and Attitudinal Variables on Perception of Alcohol

Multiple R = .35**
Multiple R^2 = 13%

Impact of selected demographic and attitudinal variables on perception of alcohol (standardized Beta weights)

Marijuana perceived as problem	.32**
Legalize marijuana	.04
Alcoholics are different	-.13**
Protestant	.01
Democrats	-.04
Voted 1972	.02
Education	-.03
Religiosity	.07**
Age	-.03
Sex	-.06

*p>.05
**p>.01

Discussion
To what extent do these findings support a public health, systems-based paradigm? The findings presented in Figure 1 and Table 1 are suggestive of this model. Most respondents perceive alcohol as a problematic substance. They also do not see the alcoholic as different from others. These two beliefs are closely linked. Indeed, even when other respondent beliefs and characteristics are taken into account, perception of the "alcoholic" remains one of the most important predictors of views toward alcohol. These findings are just the opposite of what might be expected based on a medical model.

Views on marijuana appear to parallel social thought on alcohol. These respondents overwhelmingly believe any use of marijuana is problematic. There is little reliable indication of their peception of the marijuana user. The scale is weak and responses only suggest a state of flux or uncertainty. Views on marijuana are closely related to those held about alcohol. The best predictor of perception of alcohol as a problematic substance is a belief that marijuana is a problematic substance.

Interestingly, but not surprisingly, this study indicates that views on alcohol and marijuana may also parallel incidence and prevalence trends. Young males who are better educated, Democrats, and not religiously active are most likely to subscribe to the medical model for both alcohol and marijuana. These same individuals are also most likely to use these substances in greater quantities (e.g., Cahalan, 1970; National Institute on Drug Abuse, 1980).

Kuhn (1970) suggests that with changes in paradigms come changes in potential solutions. Do these data suggest changes in public opinion on policy related to perceptions of alcohol and marijuana? A public health model would place increasing emphasis on limiting access or supply in the hopes of decreasing the overall consumption of alcohol or marijuana. Lower rates of use would then result in fewer individuals using the substance problematically (Beauchamp, 1980). This sample clearly approves limitations on access to marijuana. However, this finding may merely represent the continuation of our earlier prohibitory, moralistic policy. Unfortunately, in this study there are no measures of support for limiting access to alcohol through taxation or age restriction.

Yet, while a public health paradigm clearly emphasizes the supply side of the equation, no policy could ignore the demand side. A systems-oriented approach might expend greater efforts on prevention compared to a medical approach. It is not clear what implications a public health approach holds for those individuals considered "alcoholic." This sample clearly continues to perceive alcoholism treatment in terms of a medical model, which has a number of advantages over the moral model it replaced. Shifting to a public health model could also provide advantages to those treated. If the heavy drinker is no different from others and alcohol is a problematic substance for all, then problematic drinkers might have a different view of themselves. These individuals might also be less stigmatized by

society and might find it easier to shed their deviant label.
Although the prevailing paradigm may be changing, the response of this sample is tenuous at best. The findings presented here do not truly indicate that the recommendations of this sample follow a systems-oriented philosophy of limitations on access, preventive measures, and a less stigmatizing, perhaps more holistic, approach to treatment. This may be due to the weakness of the available measures and/or the age of these data.

Since 1974, it does appear that public opinion on alcohol and marijuana is changing. Concern over intoxicated drivers and the impact of alcohol in the workplace seems to have increased (e.g., the rising numbers of employee assistance programs and the increasing political power of those lobbying for stricter "drunk driving" laws). Several states have raised the legal drinking age in an effort to limit access. These data do suggest that individuals most likely to use alcohol and marijuana will be most opposed to these policies.

Finally, Kuhn (1970) notes that when paradigms shift, research questions also shift. New subjects for investigation appear that would not have been considered under the old framework. A shift to a systems-oriented public health paradigm would result in future research aimed at exploring the impact on consumption of various levels of taxation, age restrictions, and other efforts to manipulate supply levels. One of the largest gaps in our knowledge is the lack of current information on the extent to which the public supports policies limiting access to alcohol. Clearly, a greater emphasis would be placed on prevention research. Research on problematic drinkers would expand to include the impact of numerous systems outside the individual. Finally, as this research indicates, studies of public opinion and social thought on alcohol will have to refine their measures. The findings presented here are relatively weak and are only suggestive of the conclusions discussed above.

REFERENCES

ADAMHA
    1981   Reagan Aid: Broaden Attack on Drug Abuse. *ADAMHA News* 7(25):1.
Beauchamp, D. E.
    1980   *Beyond Alcoholism.* Philadelphia: Temple University Press.
Brody, J. E.
    1976   Study on Alcoholics Called Misleading. *New York Times*, June 10:1.
Brody, J. E.
    1980a   Alcoholic Study Supports Finding That Some Can Resume Drinking. *New York Times*, January 25:14.
Brody, J. E.
    1980b   Drinking Problem Dispute. *New York Times*, January 30:19.

Cahalan, D.
1970   *Problem Drinkers.* San Francisco: Jossey Bass.
Cahalan, D., I. H. Cissin, and H. M. Crossley
1969   *American Drinking Practices.* New Brunswick, N.J.:   Rutgers Center of
       Alcohol Studies.
Cahalan, D., and R. Room
1974   *Problem Drinking Among American Men.* New Brunswick, N.J.:   Rutgers
       Center of Alcohol Studies, Monograph No. 7.
Conrad, P., and J. W. Schneider
1980   *Deviance and Medicalization.* St. Louis: C. V. Mosby.
Haberman, P., and J. Scheinberg
1969   Public Attitudes Toward Alcoholism as an Illness.   *American Journal of
       Public Health* 59:1209–1216.
Kuhn, T. S.
1970   *The Structure of Scientific Revolutions.* Chicago: The University of
       Chicago Press.
Levine, H. G.
1978   The Discovery of Addiction: Changing Conceptions of Habitual
       Drunkenness in America. *Journal of Studies on Alcohol* 39:143–174.
Linsky, A. S.
1970   The Changing Public Views of Alcoholism. *Quarterly Journal of Studies on
       Alcohol* 31:692–704.
Martin, E., D. McDuffee, and S. Presser
1981   *Sourcebook of Harris National Surveys: Repeated Questions 1963–1976.*
       University of North Carolina, Chapel Hill: Institute for Research in Social
       Science.
Mulford, H., and D. Miller
1964   Measuring Public Acceptance of the Alcoholic as a Sick Person.   *Quarterly
       Journal of Studies on Alcohol* 25:314–323.
National Commission on Marijuana and Drug Abuse
1972   *Drug Abuse in America: Problem in Perspective.* Washington, D.C.:   U.S.
       Government Printing Office.
National Institute on Drug Abuse
1980   *Marijuana and Health.* Washington, D.C.:   U.S. Government Printing
       Office.
Reiss, K.
1977   Public Acceptance of the Disease Concept of Alcoholism.   *Journal of
       Health and Social Behavior* 18:338–344.
Singh, B. K., L. D. Knezek, and L. D. Adams
1979   Changes in Reactions to Deviance: The Issue of Legalization of Marijuana.
       Journal of Drug Issues 9:498–510.
Watts, T. D.
1982   Three Traditions in Social Thought on Alcoholism. *International Journal
       of the Addictions* 17:1231–1239.

THE SOCIAL THOUGHT OF ALCOHOLICS

Ernest Kurtz
Linda Farris Kurtz

Concern about alcoholism historically involves concern about the social thought of alcoholics. Alcoholics Anonymous "works" by changing the social thought of its members. Yet, also for historical reasons, large differences exist between the wisdom-orientation of the social thought of Alcoholics Anonymous and the knowledge-orientation that characterizes the social thought of modern professionals. Empirical testing of these historical generalizations suggests that understanding those differences is essential to establishing rapport between treatment professionals and AA members.

Despite abundant attention to alcoholism, most social thought on alcoholics tends to be monothematic regarding the social thought *of* alcoholics. For it is precisely the *social thought* of alcoholics that commentators on the phenomenon of alcoholism consistently condemn—whether explicitly or implicitly, whether in theological or in psychological terms.

After establishing that context, what follows will detail its development within the history of American social thought on alcoholism. Exploring that development will suggest the thesis that the fellowship and program of Alcoholics Anonymous not only represents the first clear articulation of the social thought *of* alcoholics, but that AA "works" precisely *by* changing the social thought of its alcoholic members. After examining that cognitive change and its foundation, and after noting recent apparent threats to the AA process, this paper concludes by reporting research that investigates the extent of conscious ideological conflict between members of Alcoholics Anonymous and community mental health professionals who work in the field of alcoholism treatment.

Historical Context

First, to establish the context—the pattern of condemnation of precisely the social thought *of* alcoholics. Examining only the American history of this topic reveals that from colonial times to the present, the alcoholic[1] has been denounced as "lacking all concern for others," as "exquisitely individualistic," and as "morbidly self-centered" (Mather, 1673; Whitefield, 1740; Strecker, 1937;

Ernest Kurtz received his Ph.D. in the History of American Civilization from Harvard University in 1978. He is the author of *Not-God: A History of Alcoholics Anonymous*, of *Shame and Guilt: An Historical Perspective for Professionals*, and of "Why A.A. Works: The Intellectual Significance of Alcoholics Anonymous." Currently a resident of Chicago, Illinois, he travels to present workshops on relationships between Alcoholics Anonymous and professionals and serves as a Visiting Lecturer at the Rutgers University Summer School of Alcohol Studies.
Linda Farris Kurtz, D.P.A., is an assistant professor at the University of Chicago School of Social Service Administration. Formerly a mental health practitioner and administrator in the State of Georgia, she helped found a residential center for substance abusers. She has recently published several articles on the relationships between AA members and professionals.

Alcoholics Anonymous, 1955; Armstrong, 1958; Bateson, 1971). A deep instinct, both scholarly and popular, insists that the alcoholic's problem—whether understood as weakness or perversity, as "sickness" or as "sin"—consists not only in the failure to control his or her drinking but more deeply in some inability to relate adequately to other human beings. The list of character traits commonly predicated of alcoholics amply bears out this understanding: "proud," even "grandiose," in their "infantilism," alcoholics consistently demonstrate that they are "incapable of mature relationships" (Knight, 1937; Strecker, 1937; Armstrong, 1938; Keller, 1972).

Within this usual understanding, two fundamental paradigm shifts have nevertheless occurred, marking the historical phases of American society's understanding of alcoholism (Levine, 1978:143–144, 161–162). The first, which took place in the Revolutionary epoch and is associated with the name of Dr. Benjamin Rush, reflects the beginning of the application of modern scientific thought to the phenomenon of alcoholism. The second, inspired by Alcoholics Anonymous, represents a reintegration and reinterpretation of elements of the earlier understanding that hindsight experience suggests had been too cavalierly jettisoned.

Attitudes Rooted in Theology

Until the very end of the eighteenth century, the main body of thinkers who addressed the phenomenon of alcoholism were the clergy. Premodern in their assumptions and approach, colonial clerics defined the problem as "habitual drunkenness." Their generally Calvinist world view interpreted that condition as "sinful," for it involved the misuse of one of "God's good creatures...alcohol" (Lender & Martin, 1982:1–19).

Two aspects of habitual drunkenness rendered it especially fascinating, and especially fearsome, to these clerical observers. Theologically, as "habit," it clearly involved a key Calvinist concern—the freedom of the will (Edwards, 1754; Levine, 1978:147–151). Socially and politically, habitual drunkenness evidently endangered the ideal of community that Calvinist thought sought to establish in its role as mediator between the medieval corporate mentality and the modern ideology of liberal individualism (Cotton, 1648; Miller, 1941 & 1956; Hartz, 1955; Heimert, 1966; McNeill, 1967; May, 1976). Both aspects of Calvinist concern require deeper examination if we would understand current attitudes toward alcoholism.

Theologically, the Calvinist conception of "original sin" involved acceptance of innate human flawedness. A propensity for evil lurks deeply rooted in human nature—a satanic inclination to challenge divinity itself. This tendency expresses itself most often in the misuse of one of "God's good creatures"; and such abuse at least implies the claim to *be* "God." In the Calvinist world view, alcohol seemed ironically liable to such abuse. A benevolent God had intended it to ease the pain of being human, itself a penalty of original sin. But consumed in excess, alcohol treacherously rendered drinkers less than human even as it promised to make them more than human, thus replicating original sin itself. (Lender & Martin, 1982:1–19).

Such a theology did not lack an understanding of "addiction." In choosing thus to misuse alcohol, the willful drunkard weakened his will to resist later such choices. Although bitter remorse was an inevitable penalty of drunkenness, that "bite of conscience" could be itself eased by alcohol. The drunkard thus stood on a most slippery slope: opening the door to sin, he readily became dominated by it. His will, closed to God's grace, inevitably and increasingly chose evil (Mather, 1673; Danforth, 1710; Whitefield, 1740; Edwards, 1754; Levine, 1978). The phenomenology of alcoholism fit well American Calvinism's theological assumptions concerning human nature.

Within the Calvinist world view, of course, the social and the political were the woof to theology's warp: their interweaving constituted the very fabric of society. And again, colonial experience with alcohol use and misuse seemed to validate that understanding. Just as the Calvinist insight understood what moderns term "addiction," it recognized also the paradox of sociability—the need of human beings to be both individual and social, both separate and connected. Calvinists stood before God and among each other not only as individuals uniquely redeemed but as members of covenanted communities (Winthrop, 1630; Cotton, 1648; Miller, 1941 & 1956).

To lose sight of either aspect of the paradox was dangerous. Especially in America, colonial Calvinists became almost obsessed with the problem of community—with sustaining the paradox. Their communities were extremely vulnerable. Both Native American resentment of the white man's ongoing exploitation and the constant danger that European rivalries would be fought out on American shores impelled thinkers already so inclined by their theology to insist upon the value and virtue of community. They therefore sought to protect and to foster the kind of relationships that enhanced each individual's ability and willingness to contribute value and virtue to the community.

Alcohol itself seemed to serve the purposes of community. Consumed in moderation, it enabled work by alleviating the pains of toil; it also fostered sociability by warming and opening the hearts of men to one another (Keller, 1979; Lender & Martin, 1982). Consumed to excess, however, as by the habitual drunkard, alcohol produced the opposite effects. The drunkard, if not unable to labor at all, produced shoddy work. Even more threatening to community were the drunkard's bellicosity and abandonment of inhibitions. The line between warmth and heat in social gatherings may be thin and ill-defined, but colonial observers had ample evidence that drunkenness did not promote the deeper purposes of community. Habitual drunkards, then, jeopardized not only their own salvation but their community's very survival.

Shift from the Theological to the Secular
The dawn of the Revolutionary epoch brought changes in both theological and social assumptions. Two names signal their import. Anthony Benezet, a Quaker reformer, published in 1774 the first American pamphlet urging total abstinence from distilled beverages (Benezet, 1774). Quaker theology, although Calvinist in origin, contained the seed of greater trust in human goodness: sufficiently enlightened, an individual *could* abstain. An even deeper theological revolution, as well as a more profound shift in social thought, appears in the thought and writings of Dr. Benjamin Rush (1784).

Rush, signer of the Declaration of Independence and "the father of American psychiatry," is generally hailed also as the formulator of the modern disease concept of alcoholism (Levine, 1978:151–153; Lender & Martin, 1982:37–40). He is correctly credited with creating a new paradigm that gave birth to the modern understanding of "habitual drunkenness"—identifying the causal agent as spiritous liquors, describing the drunkard's compulsion as loss of control over drinking behavior, declaring the condition a disease, and prescribing total abstinence as the only cure (Levine, 1978:152).

But Dr. Rush's contribution signified more. His new paradigm for habitual drunkenness was but a corollary of a deeper ideological shift that occurred at the end of the eighteenth century: the transition from an inherently religious to an explicitly secular paradigm (Gay, 1969). Although prolonged in its development and uneven in its dominance, the germ of this new world view was securely in place by the time Rush wrote. Two aspects of it, patent in Rush, are relevant to the change in social thought that he reflected and furthered.

The theology of the Age of Enlightenment tended to view human nature as essentially good, as corrupted only from the outside (Gay, 1969; May, 1976). Although generally accepting human perfection as unattainable, it emphasized the *perfectibility* of human individuals. Socially, Enlightenment abolition of class-based distinctions and rejection of hierarchical ideas of "proper place" vaunted the individual over the community in a way that resolved the ancient paradox of sociability by sacrificing any concept of community that viewed it as more than mere aggregation. Liberal individualism became the cornerstone of all subsequent social thought, especially in America (Unger, 1975).

Society-wide adoption of the new philosophy of course proceeded slowly and unevenly. Glimmerings can be detected as early as 1662, but it attained hegemony only in the Jacksonian era—the period beginning in the 1830s that has been aptly labeled "Freedom's Ferment" (Tyler, 1944; Meyers, 1960; Douglas 1977). During that decade, as Levine (1978:154–157) has cogently demonstrated, virtually the whole of the modern understanding of alcoholism that would a century and a quarter later be associated with the name of Jellinek (1960) was developed and established. That understanding fueled the nineteenth-century Temperance Movement at least until the advent of the Anti-Saloon League in the 1890s (Gusfield, 1963:99–110; Timberlake, 1963; Sinclair, 1964:83–105; Lender & Martin, 1982:126–128). Physicians, following the lead of Dr. Rush, were among its most prominent adherents. Insofar as any identifiable group opposed the understanding, it was to be found among a minority of the clergy (Levine, 1978:158)[2]—their minority status reflecting the strange anomaly that was nineteenth-century American mainstream religion.

As many commentators have noted, nineteenth-century American Evangelicalism, severed from its Calvinist roots by frontier revivalism no less than by the Jeffersonian revolution, entered into a strange marriage with modern liberalism (Smith, 1957; Mead, 1963; McLoughlin, 1968 & 1978; Boles, 1972). Although retaining some Calvinist trappings, this new ideology tended to blend secular and religious assumptions in a uniquely modern way. Evil existed in the world, perhaps at times even infecting human beings; the task of the American Christian—both as American and as Christian—was to triumph over that evil by fostering Reform that carried on the redemption of Christ. "As He died to make men holy, let us live to make men free"[3]: "The Battle Hymn of the Republic" aptly summarizes this insight and its thrust, up to and including even parts of the early twentieth-century "Social Gospel." (Howe, 1862; Rauschenbusch, 1907; Hopkins, 1940; Handy, 1966; Ahlstrom, 1967).

Largely because of its Christian gilding, the Reform orientation emphasized an attitude that had remained only implicit in Dr. Rush's understanding: "an essentially sympathetic view of the drunkard's plight" (Levine, 1978:159). The fraternal-group style of organization, pioneered by the Washingtonians but continued by others after that association's demise, facilitated and guaranteed such an approach—even in an increasingly individualistic society (Maxwell, 1950; Brown, 1976; Tyrell, 1979:57–59; Lender & Martin, 1982:74–79). That sympathy represented a carryover from the premodern, even pre-Calvinist understanding. It marked acceptance of the "sinner" even while decrying the "sin"—an acceptance rooted in the sense that all were, at least potentially, "sinners" (Przywara, 1958).

Because it derived from a premodern understanding, because it apparently denied individual responsibility for control, such a "sympathetic view of the drunkard's plight" could not survive the onslaught of Progressive thought that signaled the penultimate modernization of American society (Kolko, 1963; Wiebe, 1967; Buenker, 1973; Berman, 1982). Led by the Anti-Saloon League, the Temperance Movement shifted from a concern for "assimilative reform" to the imposition of legislative coercion (Gusfield, 1963; Lender & Martin, 1982).

Although aspects of it were to prove ironic, the shift itself was hardly subtle. The pragmatic politics of the time seemed to require holding up to scorn not only alcohol the substance and the places and persons who dealt in its trade, but also the drinker and especially the alcoholic (Levine, 1978:161–162; Wittet, 1979). Physicians, engrossed not only with the recent discovery of germs and with newly developed medical technologies but also by the imperatives of establishing a protective monopoly over the practice of medicine, lost patience with "diseases" not amenable to their newly emerging skills (Starr, 1982:112–144, 166–169). At precisely the time when Progressive Federal agencies were discovering a whole host of new addictive drugs, the Temperance Movement lost the sense that habitual drunkenness involved an addiction—the insight that had been its main contribution to social thought on alcoholism (Clark, 1976).

Despite the apparent ironies, that outcome seems inevitable in historical hindsight. The modernizing thrust of progressivism, of which the movement that led to the eventual passage of the Prohibition Amendment was a part, marked the triumph of liberal individualism in American society. The virtual omnipotence of human will was an essential assumption of this ideology (White, 1957; Noble, 1958; May 1959; Cawelti, 1965; Marcell, 1974; Gilbert, 1977, Rothman, 1978). To phrase it in the moralism so characteristic of the Progressive world view: because some human beings so obviously *could* control their drinking, all humans *should* do so. If some as obviously *could not* exercise such control, then all *should not* drink alcohol at all. The totalitarian monism inherent in the world view of Progressive liberal individualism rendered any other conclusion impossible. If all humans could not control their drinking equally, then equality required that all should refrain from drinking equally. The logic of the Eighteenth Amendment, from this point of view, was irrefutable.

The Great Depression and the 1930s brought not so much different assumptions as a change in some social implications of political reality. Both domestically and internationally, events challenged the very foundations of the ideology of liberal individualism. It is impressive testimony to the bankruptcy of thought in the United States of the time that the leaders of the Association Against the Prohibition Amendment became the bellwethers of the most virulently conservative opposition to Franklin D. Roosevelt's New Deal (Engelmann, 1979; Kyvig, 1979). Irony wears many faces.

Thus, the modern philosophy of liberal individualism did not die in the 1930s. Aptly, given the sources and the nature of many of the attacks upon that ideology, a new generation of intellectuals joined an older established coterie of professionals as its primary adherents and defenders (Bledstein, 1976; Lasch, 1977 & 1978; Rothman, 1980). Two occurrences of the mid-1930s thus combine to signal the continuing ambivalence rooted in all of American social thought on alcoholism. Even as professionals were dedicating an institution to furbishing the social scientific approach to alcoholism, a fellowship of alcoholics was formulating a program that marked recovery of the older tradition that attended to the social thought of alcoholics.

Both the Research Council on Problems of Alcohol—which later became the Yale and in time the Rutgers Center of Alcohol Studies—and what we have come to know as "Alcoholics Anonymous" date from this period. The first, having recaptured and validated the understanding of alcoholism pioneered by Dr. Rush and prevalent in the 1830s, continues to explore with all the tools of modern science the phenomenon of alcoholism (Wilkerson, 1966; Levine, 1978:162; Keller, 1979:2826–2827). Alcoholics Anonymous, while grateful for that knowledge, of which it at times makes use, focuses its direct attention and concern upon the alcoholic. In doing so, AA embraces aspects of the premodern understanding that reflects ancient wisdom.

That division of labor and diversity of ideology has, in general, proven fruitful. Whether it can continue to be so, however, has become a real question. Before exploring that question and the problems perhaps inherent in the diversity of focus and ideology that distinguish the professional and the AA approaches, it seems appropriate to review what the historical background just outlined might teach concerning the significance and implications of the present context.

Two Paradigms

The fundamental paradigm difference in American social thought on alcoholism may be conceptualized variously. If "focus on alcoholism—focus on the alcoholic" seems too glib and even fuzzy, as it no doubt is, then our historical review proffers another suggestion. There are available two models. Neither is "pure" nor clearly defined, and the attempt to name either is fraught with hazards—but let us try. At least part of the colonial insight, which lasted well into the nineteenth century and has been resurrected by Alcoholics Anonymous, seems most aptly labeled "premodern," "traditional," "perennial," or even "religious." Dr. Rush's understanding, as honed by Channing (1836) and Woodward (1838), and refurbished in contemporary dress by Jellinek (1960) and his multitudinous successors, is by contrast "modern," "secular," "scientific," and imbued with the assumptions of liberal individualism (Levine, 1978:166; Lender & Martin, 1982:186–190).

But labeling, even if it be understood as other than sophisticated name-calling, by itself sheds little light on the issues involved. We must look to the *content* of these two fundamentally diverse paradigms and, especially, to the two very different understandings that lie at their roots.

The first concerns the relationship between the individual and community. The premodern understanding viewed the individual *first*, but not only, as a part of some larger whole (Huxley, 1938; Berman, 1981; Wilber, 1983; Whitfield, 1984).

Its insight might be phrased: "There is something greater than the self, of which the self is or yearns to be part." The modern scientific understanding is first and ultimately individualistic. Self as essentially discrete is its starting point; and self attains individual fulfillment only over against all that is outside the self, over against community. There is little room in the modern world view for a "power greater than the self" with which one has a *complementary* relationship (Bateson, 1971).

The second facet of content significant in this context concerns each paradigm's understanding of human nature—that is, of the *meaning* of being human. The modern world view regards the human individual as inherently "good"—or at least as in no way inherently "bad." Trusting one's self is the hallmark of modern thought (Kant, 1784; Lasch, 1978; Hartle, 1983). Although value terms are explicitly eschewed, moderns understand being human as being, at least potentially, "good." If humans act badly, it is because of the influence of something that remains essentially outside the core itself. The Rush-Jellinek "disease-concept of alcoholism" well replicates and conveys this understanding, as do all efforts that assume the desirability of "controlled drinking" (Heather & Robertson, 1981).

The premodern or perennial tradition embraces a vision that sees the human as essentially limited and therefore as *mixed*. It views "being human" as being both "beast" and "angel," as participating in infinity while remaining essentially finite, as an ultimately mysterious mixture of "not" and "God." This perspective sees being human as a paradox (Goldmann, 1964). Rejecting the distinction between fact and value (MacIntyre, 1981; Kolakowski, 1982), traditional thought presents the *reality* of "being human" as precisely the conjunction of "good" and "evil" in the same "self." In this understanding, alcoholism is a "sickness" in the same way that "sin" is a sickness: the alcoholic does not "have" it—he *is* it. To be an alcoholic, then, is *not* to "have alcoholism": it is to *be* an alcoholic (E. Kurtz, 1979 & 1982).

From that brief sketch of the deeper philosophical differences involved in the two paradigms, it seems clear that the modern disease-concept of alcoholism and the traditional understanding of alcoholism as "sickness" barely touch. That does not, of course, mean that *both* may not be valid. Indeed, it is one thesis of this paper that each is legitimate, within its own assumptions.

But the difference between those assumptions, combined with the similarity of their vocabularies, means that misunderstandings and conflict can all too readily occur between their adherents. It is perhaps a wonder of our time, and it certainly says much about the nature of social thought on alcoholism, that the Center for Alcohol Studies and many researchers into alcoholism work so productively—albeit warily—with members of Alcoholics Anonymous, whose primary, indeed only, concern is the alcoholic.

What happens at the Center for Alcohol Studies, the nature and assumptions of modern research into alcoholism, need hardly be detailed for readers of this book. What happens in the fellowship and program of Alcoholics Anonymous, on the other hand, likely requires precisely such detailed analysis. That has been attempted, at depth, elsewhere (E. Kurtz, 1982 & forthcoming). Here, the core of that analysis can perhaps best and most briefly be presented by suggesting that AA effects in its members precisely a cognitive change in their social thought. The social thought *of* alcoholics thus becomes the most important reality in the "therapy" of Alcoholics Anonymous.

As even sympathetic observers have frequently pointed out, Alcoholics Anonymous contains a "theology" (Bateson, 1971) or expresses an "ideology" (Blumberg, 1977; Taylor, 1979; Tournier, 1979). In its own terms, AA presents its program as a "way of life," and any "way of life" naturally includes and involves a *way of thinking* (Alcoholics Anonymous, 1953:15 & 1955:23).

The way of life, and therefore the way of thinking, taught by and fostered within Alcoholics Anonymous emphasizes perennial *wisdom*, preferring its insights to the approach that characterizes modern "knowledge" (E. Kurtz, forthcoming). Two understandings of wisdom hold special place in the AA way of life: sensitivity to self-as-part and acceptance of "being human" as a *mixed* experience, a paradoxical condition. Undergirding these understandings rests the fundamental insight of wisdom: all human reality is essentially limited.

Wisdom's point of view is most evident in Alcoholics Anonymous in its corollaries: the centrality of "humility," the emphasis on "gratitude," and the modality of "telling stories." Each signals the core acceptance of fundamental limitation. Within Alcoholics Anonymous, members learn to think from and within this point of view of traditional wisdom. As the corollaries hint, this new way of thinking, although applied first to their relationship with alcohol, necessarily extends also to AA members' relationships with all other reality—especially in that reality's *human* aspects. This *is* "social thought."

The concept of *wisdom* as a "way of thinking" that has special reference to "social thought" can, of course, be only touched upon in this brief article. It nevertheless requires at least that brief mention; the insight that "self" is *part*, that limitation is of the essence of the individual human condition, bears far-reaching implications for one's relationships with other human individuals. For members of Alcoholics Anonymous, then, it is a change in "social thought" that *is* the gateway to sobriety.

The distinction between "modern knowledge" and traditional "wisdom" may also prove useful in another way. Recent events have led to tensions that seem to be testing the AA insight. Their outcome may prove especially revealing of the possible limits of AA's rooting in wisdom. Wisdom, recall, is conscious first and especially of *limits*. For roughly a decade now, ongoing changes in the field of alcoholism treatment have increasingly impinged upon Alcoholics Anonymous, threatening AA's own sense of limitation from two directions: the restriction of its fellowship to the single purpose of helping alcoholics and the acceptance enshrined in AA's "Big Book" that its program "surely has no monopoly on" and indeed may *not* be "the last word" in helping alcoholics (Alcoholics Anonymous, 1955:xxi).

First came the problem of "other problems"—hardly new in AA history, but given new and different impetus by the development of the concept of "chemical dependency" (E. Kurtz, 1979). Can the "identification" required for recovery be achieved and fostered if, increasingly, more and more who attend meetings of Alcoholics Anonymous announce that their primary problem is not alcohol but other mood-changing drugs? AA's historic solution to this problem has been the encouragement of other groups, such as Narcotics Anonymous, to use the Twelve Step program within their own contexts. But where will this stop? Do abusers of the so-called minor tranquilizers identify most readily with those whose problem was with illegal drugs? If not, must they form "Valium-takers Anonymous"? The problem/opportunity of *identification*, its foundation and its limitations, is likely to be a critical one for Alcoholics Anonymous for some time to come.

Second, the increasing prominence of professionals of various sorts in the field of alcoholism treatment doubly menaces AA's sense of limitation from the opposite direction. In settings such as general hospitals, professional dominance threatens to co-opt Alcoholics Anonymous to the modern world view by treating its program as simply another modality of treatment (Pattison, 1977; Vaillant, 1983). Other professionals criticize AA as "obscurantist" and therefore an impediment to research in treatment and to the development of new treatments—certainly not a new phenomenon in AA history, but one that appears currently on the increase (Cain, 1963 & 1965; Kalb & Propper, 1976; Tournier, 1979).

Traditionally, and from its very origins, Alcoholics Anonymous has welcomed cooperation with all professionals—if for no other reason than as sources of possible future referrals. Members also readily reply to professional criticisms by suggesting that they are misguided: because AA is a "program of *recovery*," it cannot be in conflict with any method of "treatment." Alcoholics Anonymous, this argument runs, stands ready to "cooperate" with *any* program of treatment (Alcoholics Anonymous, 1982). Increasingly, however, some professionals in the field seem to find it difficult to cooperate with the AA way of life (Demone, 1979; Goodwin, 1979; Moore, 1979; Rosenberg 1979; Sobell & Sobell, 1979; Tournier, 1979). Accurately, even if obscurely, they recognize that the AA way of thinking is not that of science. The modern scientific approach to any problem values change: it advances by the testing of new hypotheses. Most AA members, viewing alcoholism as a matter of life and death for the alcoholic, understandably resist the testing of new strategies that seem too cavalierly to abandon approaches that experience has proven valuable. In this, of course, they are again reflecting the tradition of wisdom, which—in contrast with the approach of knowledge—gives the benefit of the doubt to that which has endured over time rather than to that which seems attractive mainly because, as new and different, it bodes well for promotions and grants.

Empirical Findings

A recent research effort undertook to investigate and to measure this potential for ideological conflict between members of Alcoholics Anonymous and professionals who work in the field of alcoholism treatment. The inquiry sought to establish an empirical base for evaluating the hypothesis that there exist two cognitive paradigms about alcoholism—one characterizing the thought of alcoholics who have adopted the AA way of thinking, the other deriving from the scientific approach that characterizes the modern professional.

The research design comprised two phases. The first involved sending questionnaires both to professionals who worked in alcoholism treatment centers and to members of Alcoholics Anonymous. The questionnaires sought to measure agreement or disagreement with statements that reflected ideological contrasts. The second mode of inquiry entailed interviewing members of both populations, basing the sample chosen for interview on diverse patterns of interaction between the two groups, revealed by the questionnaires. In the course of these open-ended interviews, each respondent was asked whether he or she thought AAs and professionals had different "ways of thinking." Forty-two professionals and thirty-one AA members returned questionnaires; fifteen professionals and eleven members of Alcoholics Anonymous gave personal interviews (L. Kurtz; 1983; L. Kurtz, 1984).

Construction of the questionnaire's Likert-scaled statements required defining clearly the characteristics both of the professional approach and of the way of thinking implied in the AA way of life. Although that process is described more fully and in greater detail in another place (L. Kurtz, 1983; L. Kurtz, 1984), the considerations underlying the questionnaire's ideology scale can be summarized briefly here.

Values, beliefs, and ideologies seen as implicit in professional thought were extracted from the sociological literature on professionalism (Vollmer & Mills, 1966; Lieberman, 1970, Bledstein, 1976; Larson, 1977). Further, because professionals have both informed and been formed by the values of bureaucratic organization—the organizational structure that dominates modern society—the scale also drew on the literature studying that phenomenon (Weber, 1921:983, 988; J. Rothman, 1974:160–174; Larson, 1977:xviii; Perrow, 1979:50–55). Based on these sources, the scale characterized professional ideology as valuing scientific investigation, rational (secular) knowledge, objectivity, social and hierarchical control, expansion, efficiency, and rational-legal authority.

As the first part of this article has discussed, the way of thinking encouraged with Alcoholics Anonymous differs from modern, bureaucratic ideology in several ways. AA members tend to view personal experience as more valuable than data acquired scientifically; for them, mutuality and identification supersede detachment and objectivity as desiderata enabling effective communication. Relationships between members are egalitarian rather than hierarchical; AA's self-concept as "fellowship" signals the absence of and even an aversion to legal authority, and thus its members are controlled by their personal understanding of AA's Steps and Traditions and by the "group conscience" of each individual AA group. Further, AA members deem efficiency, in the sense of maximizing output by serving greater numbers, less important than the identification gained by sharing one's own story with one other human being. The fellowship and its members also reject organizational expansion, choosing to limit their efforts to helping alcoholics and therefore avoiding all political involvement.

Questionnaire statements sought to assess the degree to which respondents valued the following contrasting dimensions of thought: efficiency (in the sense of maximization) as opposed to the optimization attained by individual identification; organizational expansion as opposed to single-purposed limitation; objectivity as opposed to mutuality; formal authority as opposed to relative anarchy; the benefit of expert leadership as opposed to participatory validation; valuing the new and different as opposed to the traditional and time-proven; the goal of achieving control as opposed to the desirability of giving up the effort to control.

The responses revealed significant differences in four of the seven contrasts. AA members highly valued limitation, mutuality, participatory validation, and the traditional. Intercorrelations of the scale item responses showed that only the reactions to the efficiency and the control statements did not correlate with the other responses. Both AAs and professionals valued efficiency and control highly, at least as the questionnaire reflected those understandings (L. Kurtz, 1983:125–127, 238). These findings led to a tentative conclusion that professionals and AAs hold somewhat antithetical views.

The second phase of the investigation sustained that conclusion. Interviews with fifteen professionals and eleven AA members in three communities inquired about cognitive differences in a more open-ended fashion. The question, "Do you think AA members and professionals think differently?" produced affirmative responses from ten of the eleven AA members and from nine of the fifteen professionals.

The interviewees offered varied responses about the nature of the difference between the two ways of thinking. Many in both groups spontaneously identified aspects of the AA and the professional paradigms that this paper has discussed. For example, one AA member replied, "Professionals are on top; they do all the helping. In AA we help each other." Another commented, "Professionals think alcoholism is a thing that can be cured. It's not; it's a way of living that comes from erroneous beliefs."

One professional with a theological background responded, "In some ways, [AAs] don't take the disease concept seriously. This is just a feeling I have, but in some ways I agree more with them than with the medical model." Another professional gave the most typical response: "Their suffering has made them [AAs] more spiritually aware. They live each day to the fullest instead of just pissing it away." Only one of the professionals who agreed that a different way of thinking existed expressed a negative attitude toward AA. He said, "That's one of the complaints about them. They're locked into one rigid system[of thought]."

Conclusion

If their own stories are to be believed, the most outstanding difference between actively drinking and soberly recovering alcoholics consists precisely in their social thought—in the attitudes they display toward human relationships and especially in their interpretations of their own relationships with, and obligations to, others.

Cursory observation of that difference suggests a disturbing hypothesis: the ways in which the social thought of sober alcoholics differs from that of drinking alcoholics seem to parallel the ways in which the assumptions of members of Alcoholics Anonymous differ from the assumptions adhered to by many modern professionals.

Initial empirical research tends to validate that hypothesis. Whether this observation has more to say about the social thought of alcoholics or the social thought of modern professionals, it seems best to leave the reader to decide.

NOTES

1. Although especially the early literature refers most often to "habitual drunkards" and "inebriates," this paper will use only the term "alcoholic" to signify the people concerned.
2. Although Levine's treatment and interpretation of the Reverend John E. Todd reveals insufficient appreciation of the complexity of the decline of Calvinist insight in the nineteenth century, his basic point at this place supports the argument developed here.
3. In the original version of this concluding line, the fifth last word read "die." The present paper is not the place to enter the argument over whether or not it was Mrs. Howe herself who changed the word to "live" at the end of the War of the Southern Rebellion.

REFERENCES

Ahlstrom, Sydney E.
1967 *Theology in America*. Indianapolis: Bobbs-Merrill.

Alcoholics Anonymous
1939 *Alcoholics Anonymous*. New York: Works Publishing.

Alcoholics Anonymous
1953 *Twelve Steps and Twelve Traditions*. New York: A.A. World Services.

Alcoholics Anonymous
1955 *Alcoholics Anonymous*. 2d ed. New York: A.A. World Services.

Alcoholics Anonymous
1982 *C.P.C. Workbook*. New York: A.A. World Services.

Armstrong, John
1958 The Search for the Alcoholic Personality. *Annals of American Academy of Political Science* 135(Jan.) 40–47.

Bateson, Gregory
1971 The Cybernetics of "Self": A Theory of Alcoholism, *Psychiatry* 34(1): 1–18.

Benezet, Anthony
1774 *Remarks on the Nature and Bad Effects of Spiritous Liquors*. Philadelphia: n.p.

Berman, Marshall
1982 *All That Is Solid Melts Into Air*. New York: Simon & Schuster.

Berman, Morris
1981 *The Reenchantment of the World*. Ithaca: Cornell.

Bledstein, Burton J.
1976 *The Culture of Professionalism*. New York: Norton.

Blocker, Jack S., Jr.
1979 "The Modernity of Prohibitionists: An Analysis of Leadership Structure and Background." In *Alcohol Reform and Society*, edited by Jack S. Blocker, Jr., 149–170. Westport, Conn.: Greenwood.

Blumberg, Leonard
1977 The Ideology of a Therapeutic Social Movement: Alcoholics Anonymous. *Journal of Studies on Alcohol* 38(Nov.): 2122–2143.

Buenker, John D.
1978 *Urban Liberalism and Progressive Reform*. New York: Norton.

Boles, John B.
1972 *The Great Revival 1787–1805*. Lexington, Ky.: Univ. of Kentucky.

Brown, Richard D.
1976 *Modernization*. New York: Hill & Wang.

Cain, Arthur H.
1963 Alcoholics Anonymous: Cult or Cure? *Harper's* 226 (Feb.): 48–52.

Cain, Arthur H.
1965 Alcoholics *Can* Be Cured—Despite A.A., *Saturday Evening Post* 237(Sept.): 6, 8.

Cawelti, John G.
1965   *Apostles of the Self-Made Man.* Chicago: Univ. of Chicago.
Channing, William
1836   Annual Address Delivered before the Massachusetts Temperance Society, in *Annual Report of the Massachusetts Temperance Society.* Boston: n.p.
Clark, Norman H.
1976   *Deliver Us From Evil.* New York: Norton.
Cotton, John
1648   "The Way of Congregational Churches Cleared." *John Cotton on the Churches of New England* (1968), edited by Larzer Ziff, 167–364. Cambridge, Mass.: Harvard.
Danforth, Samuel
1710   *The Woeful Effects of Drunkenness.* Boston: n.p.
Demone, Harold W., Jr.
1979   Alcoholics Anonymous as Treatment and as Ideology; Comments on the Article by R. E. Tournier. *Journal of Studies of Alcohol* 40(March): 333–335.
Douglas, Ann
1977   *The Feminization of American Culture.* New York: Knopf.
Edwards, Jonathan
1754   *The Freedom of the Will,* vol. 2 of *Works of Jonathan Edwards* (1957), ed. Paul Ramsey. New Haven, Conn.: Yale.
Engelmann, Larry
1979   "Organized Thirst: The Story of Repeal in Michigan." In *Alcohol, Reform and Society,* edited by Jack S. Blocker, Jr., 171–210. Westport, Conn.: Greenwood.
Gay, Peter
1969   *The Enlightenment: An Interpretation.* Vol 2. New York: Knopf.
Gilbert, James B.
1977   *Work Without Salvation.* Baltimore: Johns Hopkins Univ.
Goldmann, Lucien
1964   *The Hidden God.* New York: The Humanities Press.
Goodwin, Donald W.
1979   Alcoholics Anonymous as Treatment and as Ideology; Comments on the Article by R. E. Tournier. *Journal of Studies on Alcohol* 40(March): 318–319.
Gusfield, Joseph
1963   *Symbolic Crusade.* Urbana, Ill.: Univ. of Illinois.
Handy, Robert T. (ed.)
1966   *The Social Gospel in America.* New York: Oxford.
Hartle, Ann
1983   *The Modern Self in Rousseau's Confessions.* Notre Dame, Ind.: University of Notre Dame.
Hartz, Louis
1955   *The Liberal Tradition in America.* New York: Harcourt, Brace & World.

Heimert, Alan
1966   *Religion and the American Mind.* Cambridge, Mass.: Harvard.
Hopkins, C. Howard
1940   *The Rise of the Social Gospel in American Protestantism, 1865–1915.* New Haven, Conn.: Yale.
Howe, Julia Ward
1862   "The Battle Hymn of the Republic." In *The American Evangelicals, 1800–1900,* edited by William G. McLoughlin, 28–29. New York: Harper.
Huxley, Aldous
1938   *The Perennial Philosophy.* New York: Harper & Row.
Jellinek, E. M.
1960   *The Disease Concept of Alcoholism.* New Haven, Conn.: College & Univ. Press.
Kalb, Melvyn, and Morton S. Propper
1976   The Future of Alcohology: Craft or Science?   *American Journal of Psychiatry* 133(6): 641–645.
Kant, Immanuel
1784   "An Answer to the Question: 'What is Enlightenment?'"   In *Kant's Political Writings* (1970), ed. Hans Reiss; trans. H. B. Nisbet, 54–60. Cambridge: The University Press.
Keller, Mark
1972   The Oddities of Alcoholics.   *Quarterly Journal of Studies on Alcohol* 33(Dec.): 1147–1148.
Keller, Mark
1979   A Historical Overview of Alcohol and Alcoholism.   *Cancer Research* 39(July): 2822–2829.
Knight, Robert
1937   The Dynamics and Treatment of Chronic Alcohol Addiction. *Bulletin of the Menninger Clinic* 1(Nov.): 233–250.
Kolakowski, Leszek
1982   *Religion.* New York: Oxford.
Kolko, Gabriel
1963   *The Triumph of Conservatism.* Chicago: Quadrangle.
Kurtz, Ernest
1979   *Not-God:*   *A History of Alcoholics Anonymous.*   Center City, Minn.: Hazelden.
Kurtz, Ernest
1982   Why A.A. Works. *Journal of Studies on Alcohol* 43(Jan.): 38–80.
Kurtz, Ernest
forth-
coming *Way of Life/Way of Thinking.* Minneapolis: Johnson Institute.
Kurtz, Linda Farris
1983   *Cooperation Between Alcoholics Anonymous Members and Alcoholism Treatment Centers in Georgia.* Dissertation, Univ. of Georgia.   University Microfilms #83–14, 732.

Kurtz, Linda Farris
1984 Ideological Differences Between Professionals and A.A. Members. *Alcoholism Treatment Quarterly*. Vol. 1, no. 2.
Kyvig, David E.
1979 "Objection Sustained: Prohibition Repeal and the New Deal." In *Alcohol, Reform and Society*, edited by Jack S. Blocker, Jr., 211–233. Westport, Conn.: Greenwood.
Larson, Magali Sarfatti
1977 *The Rise of Professionalism*. Berkeley: Univ. of California.
Lasch, Christopher
1977 *Haven in a Heartless World*. New York: Basic Books.
Lasch, Christopher
1978 *The Culture of Narcissism*. New York: Norton.
Lender, Mark Edward, and James Kirby Martin
1982 *Drinking in America*. New York: Free Press.
Levine, Harry Gene
1978 The Discovery of Addiction. *Journal of Studies on Alcohol* 39(Jan.): 143–174.
Lieberman, Jethro K.
1970 *The Tyranny of the Experts*. New York: Walker.
MacIntyre, Alasdair
1981 *After Virtue*. Notre Dame, Ind.: Univ. of Notre Dame.
McLoughlin, William G. (ed.)
1968 *The American Evangelicals, 1800–1900*. New York: Harper.
McLoughlin, William G.
1978 *Revivals, Awakenings, and Reform*. Chicago: Univ. of Chicago.
McNeill, John
1967 *The History and Character of Calvinism*. New York: Oxford.
Marcell, David
1974 *Progress and Pragmatism*. Westport, Conn.: Greenwood.
Mather, Increase
1673 *Wo To Drunkards*. Cambridge, Mass.: n.p.
Maxwell, Milton
1950 The Washingtonian Movement. *Quarterly Journal of Studies on Alcohol* 11(Sept.): 410–451.
May, Henry F.
1959 *The End of American Innocence*. Chicago: Quadrangle.
May, Henry F.
1976 *The Enlightenment in America*. New York: Oxford.
Mead, Sidney E.
1963 *The Lively Experiment*. New York: Harper & Row.
Meyers, Marvin
1957 *The Jacksonian Persuasion*. Stanford, Calif.: Stanford Univ.
Miller, Perry
1941 "Declension in a Bible Commonwealth." In *Nature's Nation* (1967), 14–49. Cambridge, Mass.: Harvard.

Miller, Perry
1956   "Errand Into the Wilderness." In *Errand Into the Wilderness* (1964), 1–15.
       New York: Harper & Row.
Moore, Robert A.
1979   Alcoholics Anonymous as Treatment and as Ideology; Comments on the
       Article by R. E. Tournier. *Journal of Studies on Alcohol* 40(March):
       328–330.
Noble, David W.
1958   *The Paradox of Progressive Thought*. Minneapolis: Univ. of Minn.
Noble, David W.
1970   *The Progressive Mind, 1890–1917*. Chicago: Rand McNally.
Pattison, E. Mansell
1977   Ten Years of Change in Alcoholism Treatment and Delivery Systems.
       Amer.Jour. Psychiatry 134(March): 261–266.
Perrow, Charles
1979   *Complex Organizations: A Critical Essay*. Glenview, Ill.: Scott,
       Foresman.
Przywara, Erich (ed.)
1958   *An Augustine Synthesis*. New York: Harper.
Rauschenbusch, Walter
1907   *Christianity and the Social Crisis*. New York: Macmillan.
Rosenberg, Chaim M.
1979   Alcoholics Anonymous as Treatment and as Ideology; Comments on the
       Article by R. E. Tournier. *Journal of Studies on Alcohol* 40(March):
       330–333.
Rothman, David J.
1971   *Discovery of the Asylum*. Boston: Little, Brown.
Rothman, David J.
1978   "The State as Parent." In *Doing Good: The Limits of Benevolence*, by
       Willard Gaylin, Ira Glasser, Steven Marcus, and David J. Rothman, 67–96.
       New York: Pantheon.
Rothman, David J.
1980   *Conscience and Convenience*. Boston: Little, Brown.
Rothman, Jack
1974   *Planning and Organizing for Social Change*. New York: Columbia.
Rush, Benjamin
1784   *An Inquiry into the Effects of Ardent Spirits upon the Human Body and
       Mind* (8th ed., 1814). Brookfield, Mass.: n.p.
Sinclair, Andrew
1964   *Era of Excess*. New York: Harper & Row.
Smith, Timothy L.
1980   *Revivalism and Social Reform*. Baltimore: Johns Hopkins Univ.
Sobell, Mark, and Linda C. Sobell
1979   Alcoholics Anonymous as Treatment and as Ideology; Comments on the
       Article by R. E. Tournier. *Journal of Studies on Alcohol* 40(March):
       320–322.

Starr, Paul
1982   The Social Transformation of American Medicine. New York: Basic.
Strecker, Edward
1937   Some Thoughts Concerning the Psychology and Therapy of Alcoholism. Journal of Nervous and Mental Diseases 86(Aug.): 191–205.
Taylor, Mary Catherine
1977   Alcoholics Anonymous: How It Works. Dissertation, Univ. of California at San Francisco. University Microfilms #79–13, 241.
Timberlake, James
1963   Prohibition and the Progressive Movement. Cambridge, Mass.: Harvard.
Tournier, Robert E.
1979   Alcoholics Anonymous as Treatment and as Ideology. Journal of Studies on Alcohol 40(3): 230–239.
Tyler, Alice Felt
1944   Freedom's Ferment. New York: Harper & Row.
Tyrrell, Ian
1979   "Temperance and Economic Change in the Antebellum North." In Alcohol, Reform and Society, edited by Jack S. Blocker, Jr., 45–67. Westport, Conn.: Greenwood.
Unger, Roberto Mangabeira
1975   Knowledge and Politics. New York: Free Press.
Vaillant, George E.
1983   The Natural History of Alcoholism. Cambridge, Mass.: Harvard.
Vollmer, Howard M., and Donald L. Mills
1966   Professionalization. Englewood Cliffs, N.J.: Prentice-Hall.
Weber, Max
1921   "On Bureaucracy." In Economy and Society (1978), trans. Claus Wittich; ed. Guenther Ross, 956–1005. Berkeley, Calif.: Univ. of California.
Whitefield, George
1740   The Heinous Sin of Drunkenness. Philadelphia: n.p.
Whitfield, Charles L.
1984   Stress Management and Spirituality during Recovery. Alcoholism Treatment Quarterly, vol. 1, no. 1.
White, Morton
1957   Social Thought in America. Boston: Beacon.
Wiebe, Robert H.
1967   The Search for Order, 1877–1920. New York: Hill & Wang.
Wilber, Ken
1983   Eye to Eye. New York: Anchor.
Wilkerson, A. E.
1966   A History of the Concept of Alcoholism as a Disease. Dissertation, Univ. of Pennsylvania. University Microfilms #67–188.
Winthrop, John
1630   "A Modell of Christian Charity." In The Puritans: A Sourcebook of Their Writings (1965), edited by Perry Miller and Thomas H. Johnson. New York: Harper.

Wittet, George G.
1979 "Concerned Citizens: The Prohibitionists of 1883 Ohio."   In *Alcohol,
Reform and Society, edited by Jack S. Blocker, Jr., 111–147.   Westport,
Conn., Greenwood.
Woodward, Samuel B.
1838 *Essays on Asylums for Inebriates*. Worcester, Mass.: n.p.

SOCIAL THOUGHT, SOCIAL MOVEMENTS, AND ALCOHOLISM: SOME IMPLICATIONS OF AA'S LINKAGES WITH OTHER ENTITIES

Lincoln J. Fry

Social thought on alcoholism can be classified into various traditions, all of which have ignored the literature on social movements. In the instance of what is known as the disease model, critics claim the approach ultimately blames the alcoholic. The argument is presented that the social movement perspective suggests that the victim of what passes as the politics of social policy formation will be the organization Alcoholics Anonymous (AA). It is noted that some describe AA affiliations as resulting in social policy successes while others warn that professionals in the alcoholism field must rid themselves of AA's influence. The controversy surrounding the Rand Report (Armor et al., 1978) is examined in that context. The findings related to the differential treatment effectiveness of AA and professional treatment are reexamined, which indicated that the Rand study could have been interpreted as a document favorable to AA. This discussion is concerned with why AA was denied what could have been a major victory.

Recently, Watts (1982) discussed three traditions in social thought on alcoholism. The first was defined as "the moral perspective and the Prohibition movement," which stressed the evil of alcohol and its destructive properties; the second was labeled the "modern alcoholism movement" (the "disease" model of alcoholism), which stressed the alcoholic as "sick"; and the third was the "new public health perspective," which stressed the need for societal controls over alcohol. Watts emphasized that the new public health movement represents an attempt to put alcohol back into alcoholism policies. This perspective includes the notion of shared responsibility for alcohol and the alcoholic among alcohol users, abusers and nonusers.

In his discussion of the modern alcoholism movement, Watts (1982) indicated that the disease model ignores the role of alcohol and instead concentrates on alcoholism. He noted that the Alcoholics Anonymous (AA) program has grown in size and influence parallel with the disease concept of alcoholism, and *both* (AA and the disease model movement) stress the unique susceptibility of alcoholics.

Lincoln J. Fry, Ph.D. is presently Director of Sponsored Research at Loyola Marymount University, Los Angeles, California. He is also Principal Investigator for the "Effects of Overcrowding in the California Prison System" project funded by the Haynes Foundation. Besides corrections, his present research interests include suicide, substance abuse, and crime. He has previously published articles about alcohol and drug abuse treatment in such journals as *Social Problems, Sociological Quarterly, Journal of Health and Social Behavior*, and the *British Journal of Criminology*.

According to Conrad and Schneider (1980:103–105), the factors which determine that vulnerability are as follows: 1) Alcoholics have predisposing characteristics that consistently differentiate them from nonalcoholics; 2) Alcoholism is a progressive, inexorable process, progressing through fairly identifiable stages; 3) Alcoholics suffer "loss of control," which implies that if an alcoholic begins drinking, then he or she will be unable to stop; 4) There is an absolute necessity of abstinence in the treatment of alcoholics. As a result, Watts suggested that the modern alcoholism movement has created two distinct groups, alcoholics and normal drinkers, treating alcoholics as unique, separate, and particular. This process has been referred to as "blaming the alcoholic" (Beauchamp, 1980).

The purpose of this paper is to question the emphasis on the individual alcoholic as victim and to suggest that the alcoholism literature has treated AA as an organization central to social policy on alcoholism. It is the organization, not the individual alcoholic, that has been the hero or the villain in these critiques. The point is that this literature has totally neglected the body of social thought which deals with social movements, especially the implication that indigenous persons will ultimately be co-opted when they engage in cooperative ventures with more powerful professional groups. This paper takes that perspective and utilizes the initial Rand Report (Armor et al., 1978) and the subsequent follow-up study (Polich et al., 1981) to indicate how AA has been damaged and has become the victim of its linkage with other organizations.

Social Thought on Social Movements: Who Is the Victim?
The most influential theoretical approaches to the study of social movements have been provided by Smelser (1963), Gurr (1970), and Turner and Killian (1972). While they differ, they share the notion that common grievances among a deprived population represent the potential genesis for all social movements. Each holds that discontent produced by some structural configuration is a necessary, if not sufficient, condition to account for the rise of any specific social movement. Further, before collective action is possible, a generalized belief is necessary concerning, at least, the causes of discontent, and under certain conditions, the modes of redress.

Recently, theorists have stressed the need to develop more general structural theories of social processes as the basis for the study of social movements (McCarthy and Zald, 1977; Oberschall, 1973; Wilson, 1973), stressing the linkages between social movements and other entities. This perspective has become known as the resource mobilization framework, which refers to societal support and constraint of social movement development. Studies cast in that perspective are concerned with identifying the variety of resources available from external sources that may be mobilized and the degree to which movements are dependent upon external support for their success, as well as the tactics used by authorities to control or incorporate movements.

Cloward and Piven (1974) have described in detail how authorities control and co-opt disadvantaged groups. They have suggested that large scale public funding creates bureaucratic structures which become the domain of professionals and their special knowledge, a process they defined as the consolidation of expertise. The social service field has provided numerous examples of how rewards have been used to co-opt indigenous people, especially through their use as paraprofessionals (Reissman, 1965; Piven, 1974; Fry, 1976, 1977). Berman and Haug (1973) identified a major dilemma for paraprofessionals. Upward mobility within an agency may weaken the bonds between paraprofessionals and the groups from which they are drawn. Clients may resent the indigenous worker's advancement, and upwardly mobile paraprofessionals can lose a sense of identification with clients; elsewhere, Bullington et al. (1969) have documented that phenomenon in a community-based drug abuse treatment program, calling it the "purchase middle class conformity."

AA and Social Policy on Alcoholism

Blumberg (1977) has suggested that "it was not much of an exaggeration to observe that the development of a publicly funded alcoholism bureaucracy and of a community treatment personnel, with associated multidisciplinary researchers and centers for the study of 'alcohology' serves as a measure of the success of AA as a social movement" (1977:2122–2123). Schneider (1978) made a similar point when he attributed what he defined as the "success" of the spread and acceptance of the disease concept of alcoholism as a social product, resulting from the efforts of AA, the Yale Center on Alcohol Studies, and the first director of the Yale Center, E. M. Jellinek. According to Schneider, the various parties cooperated to launch a national educational campaign designed to gain acceptance for the disease concept. Schneider suggested that the success of that effort was separate and apart from the validity of the disease concept, and he stressed that acceptance represented a social accomplishment which owed its life to the efforts and vested interests of the cooperating parties.

Numerous individuals disagree with the position that AA's influence has resulted in a number of social policy successes. These critics tend to embrace two contradictory positions: either they stress that AA has failed to accept its legitimate social responsibility because of the failure to support broad social change strategies or they argue that AA has exerted undue influence, often with harmful effects for the majority of alcoholics.

The first position is apparent in Gartner and Reissman's (1977) version of what they defined as the "self-help world view." They indicated that self-help groups do not look to structural-societal solutions to social problems. They stated that "AA is concerned about the treatment of the alcoholic, not about the removal of alcohol or the societal produced stress related to the stimulation of drinking....There is a basic tendency in the self-help world view to: 1) deal with the problem at the symptom level; 2) look for small scale solutions; 3) define marginal alternatives to the major institutional caregiving system; and 4) to be broadly critical of institutions and the societal framework but not to organize a direct, rounded political attack" (1977:153).

An example of the second, contradictory position was provided by Tournier (1979) when he suggested that professionals in the alcoholism field must rid themselves of the political influence of AA and the National Council on Alcoholism. He argued that acceptance of AA's ideology represents a roadblock not only to the implementation of early intervention efforts, but to treatment innovation in general. His overview of AA and its role in policy influence regarding the treatment of alcoholism can be summarized as follows: 1) due to ideological stances which, in turn, create methodological problems, specifically the failure to cooperate with research, AA's effectiveness has not been demonstrated through proper scientific evaluation techniques; 2) despite the lack of proper evaluation, AA's suspected success with certain alcoholics has been generalized as a treatment method for the entire alcoholic population, when it is most likely effective with only certain types of alcoholics; 3) the ready acceptance of AA and its ideology by one major segment of the alcoholism treatment establishment virtually precludes early intervention strategies; 4) AA and the National Council on Alcoholism have proselytized their beliefs with such vigor that the label "alcoholic" is being applied to different kinds of drinking problems that may require different kinds of interventions.

Tournier's (1979) article generated a major debate in the literature, one which rekindled interest in the previously published Rand Report (Armor et al., 1978). This occurred because Tournier has argued that AA's major tenets, that alcoholics must accept their own loss of control over alcohol and that alcoholics cannot return to normal drinking, were primary examples of the negative results of AA's influence in the policy arena.

While all of the contributions to the subsequent debate agreed that AA was a major force in alcoholism treatment policy, whether they supported or disagreed with Tournier's (1979) position revolved around where they stood on the issue of whether alcoholics can successfully return to drinking. AA's negative stance on that point became the rallying point for both sides. Tournier had singled out Pattison et al. (1977) as the harbinger of what he defined as a revisionistic view of alcohol dependency (defined as a return of alcoholics to normal drinking), but it was the Rand Report (Armor et al., 1978) that became the focal point regarding the scientific merit of the studies concerned with a return to normal drinking by alcoholics.

The issues related to the return to normal drinking question will not be

addressed here;[1] rather, a comment in the debate provided by Moore (1979) recast
the Rand Report (Armor et al., 1978) in a very different light, and this reply is
responsible for what follows in terms of the reanalysis of the Rand data. He
stressed that both sides in the controversy surrounding the Rand Report had not
made a very good impression, especially those aligned with AA. He saw their
hysterical reaction as uncalled for, particularly because he reported that the Rand
study had suggested that better results are obtained with a mixture of AA and
professional treatment than with either alone, in which case they were about equal.
As previously suggested, the debate in the literature had been interpreted as an
attack on AA by Tournier's (1979) critics and supporters, and Moore's comment
suggested the need to reexamine the findings in that report related to treatment
effectiveness.

The Rand Report
    As Roizen (1978) has indicated, the public law that created the National
Institute on Alcohol and Alcoholism (NIAAA) required the submission of an
annual report which essentially amounted to an evaluation of the effectiveness of
services and a justification for the expenditure of funds by the agency. Since a
large proportion of NIAAA's resources were devoted to treatment delivered through
a system of federally supported alcoholism treatment centers, the effectiveness of
these centers eventually became the evaluation focus. An ongoing monitoring
system was established, which at the time of the Rand Report (Armor et al., 1978)
contained demographic, treatment, and outcome data on nearly 30,000 clients who
had entered treatment at forty-four different centers throughout the country. The
information collected by that monitoring system, along with a special eighteen-
month follow-up survey conducted in eight of the treatment centers, provided the
data for the study. Some comparisons with the general population were provided
through the use of several national surveys on drinking practices.
    The summary of the report, first published in 1976, noted that, as a group, the
alcoholics who entered treatment in the various centers were severely impaired from
excessive use of alcohol. They were found to drink nine times more alcohol than
the average person, and to experience negative behavioral consequences at a rate
nearly twelve times that for the nonalcoholic population. They were socially
impaired, with more than half unemployed and more than half separated or
divorced. They were engaged primarily in blue-collar occupations and had lower
incomes and less education than the average American (Armor et al., 1978:293).
    To paraphrase the Report's summary, despite their impaired status, clients
were found to show substantial improvement, both at six and eighteen months
following intake. While the rate of improvement was reported to be about 70
percent for several different outcome indicators (alcohol-related behaviors), social
outcomes such as employment and marital status showed much less change. That

finding was interpreted to reflect the greater emphasis by the centers on the immediate problem of alcoholic behavior (drinking). While the improvement rate was interpreted to be impressive, the report stressed that the improved clients included only a relatively small number who were long-term abstainers. About one-fourth of the clients interviewed at eighteen months had abstained for at least six months; of those who had both six-month and eighteen-month follow-ups, only 10 percent reported six months of abstention at both interviews (Armor et al., 1978:294). Consequently, the majority of improved clients in the Rand Report were either drinking moderate amounts of alcohol at levels which were suggested to be far below what could be described as alcoholic drinking, or they were engaging in alternate periods of drinking and abstention.

Because of the fact that most of the clients listed as improved were not abstaining, the Rand Report (Armor et al., 1978:294) proposed a definition of remission that included both abstention and what they referred to as "normal drinking," defined as alcoholics who consumed only moderate quantities commonly found in the general nonalcoholic population, provided no serious signs of impairment were present. Specifically, to be classifed as a "normal" drinker in the study, a person had to meet all the following criteria: 1) daily consumption of less than three ounces of alcohol; 2) typical quantities on drinking days less than five ounces; 3) no tremors reported; and 4) no serious symptoms. Serious symptoms were operationalized as frequent episodes of three or more of the following: blackouts, missing work, morning drinking, missing meals, and being drunk. "Frequent" meant three or more episodes of the other symptoms (Armor et al., 1978:98–99). According to that definition, 70 percent of the client group was in remission after treatment.

The study (Armor et al., 1978:294–295) stressed that being in remission at one follow-up period was no guarantee that the client would be in remission at a later follow-up. The crucial finding in the analysis, however, was that relapse rates for those classified as "normal" drinkers were no higher than those for longer term abstainers, even when the analysis was confined to clients who were definitely alcoholic at intake. While the study noted that its sample was small and acknowledged that the follow-up periods were relatively short, the results were interpreted to suggest the possibility that for some alcoholics "moderate drinking" is not necessarily a prelude to full relapse—some alcoholics can return to moderate drinking with no greater chance of relapse than if they abstained. Finally, the report stressed that the findings had major implications for theories of alcoholism, particularly the notion that alcoholism is caused exclusively by a physiological predisposition to addiction. While the Rand Report went on to qualify the position outlined above, both in terms of the need to verify the findings with larger samples of alcoholics as well as with longer follow-up periods, the endorsement of normal drinking for alcoholics became the major source of controversy which surrounded the Rand Report.

The Rand Report did contain information on persons who had contact with the treatment system and yet received no formal treatment; they were either screened and never appeared for treatment or made a single appearance and never returned. This meant that the study was able to compare treated and untreated clients as well as to differentiate the effects of various levels of treatment. On that basis, the study compared the results for those who entered treatment as opposed to those who did not start treatment at all. Those who entered treatment had a slightly higher remission rate than those who either had no contact or the single contact with the centers. When the treated sample was divided according to the amount of treatment, the advantage was confined to those with higher amounts of treatment. Clients with lower amounts of treatment had remission rates only slightly higher than those who received no treatment at all (Armor et al., 1978:295).

The study indicated, however, that the untreated sample had remission rates on the order of 50 percent, which obviously tempered the importance of the overall 70 percent remission rate. As Moore (1979) suggested, the report then indicated that untreated clients regularly attending AA meetings also had remission rates near 70 percent. The overall interpretation of Armor et al. (1978) was that formal treatment may play only an incremental role in the recovery from alcoholism. The study suggested that there is a natural remission from alcoholism and some alcoholics can do almost as well in AA settings as in formal inpatient and outpatient treatment settings.

The Differential Effects of AA and Professional Treatment

One of the problems which confronted the Rand Report's (Armor et al., 1978) analysis of the effects of treatment was the high percentage of clients who were also involved in other programs, with AA the most frequently cited of other treatment sources. The problem of attempting to differentiate between types of treatment was even more confounded because many of the centers included AA meetings as an adjunct to formal treatment. That institutional arrangement meant that the analysis had to consider whether some of the positive treatment effects identified could have accrued from other than the treatment provided by the centers. When the differential effects of AA and other treatment were considered, the study interpreted the results to demonstrate that the highest remission rates were found among those who received treatment from the centers or from AA. If the client received some additional treatment (not from the centers or from AA), the changes of remission were much poorer and the prognosis did not improve even if the client received high amounts of treatment from the centers. In order to examine the effects of AA more closely, the report examined those outcomes according to the regularity of AA attendance, collapsed into "no attendance," "irregular," and "regular" attendance categories, cross-tabulated according to the amount of treatment received from the centers, and dichotomized into either a "none or low" or "high" amount group. The original table is reproduced here and displayed as Table 1.

Table 1. Relationship Between Amount of Treatment and Indicators of Remission with Level of AA Attendance Controlled*

	Remission Rates (%)					
Amount of Treatment	No AA Attendance in Past Year		Irregular AA Attendance		Regular AA Attendance	
None/Low Amount Remissions	55		55		71	
Abstained 6 Months		16		12		36
Abstained One Month		8		15		35
Normal Drinking		31		28		0
Nonremissions	45		45		29	
(N)	(268)		(82)		(28)	
High Amount Remissions	83		62		84	
Abstained 6 Months		28		20		48
Abstained One Month		14		24		26
Normal Drinking		41		18		10
Nonremissions	17		38		16	
(N)	(112)		(66)		(50)	

*Reprinted from Armor et al. (1978:120)

Table 1 includes three types of remissions: clients who abstained for six months or for one month and those who drank "normally." Nonremissions were also included in the table. Armor et al. (1978:120–121) suggested that the crucial comparison in Table 1 is between regular AA participants and nonparticipants. They argued that when these two groups were compared, it is clear that the effects of AA depend on the level of treatment received from the centers. They noted that if the client received little or no formal treatment, AA made a substantial difference, raising the remission rate from 55 to 71 percent.   However, they indicated that if the client received a substantial amount of treatment, AA made no difference. Table 1 would suggest that the percentage of remissions were almost constant, 83 percent with no AA attendance as compared to 84 percent with regular AA attendance. Their conclusion was that in the absence of other treatment, AA achieves a substantial positive affect. Yet, if professional treatment is available, the impact of AA on remissions is minimal.

At that point, Armor et al. (1978:120–121) indicated that AA's philosophy advocates total abstinence and suggested that when attention was directed to that outcome, only regular AA participation appeared to make a substantial and consistent difference. They concluded that the main impact of AA was not to increase remission rates but to shift the pattern of remission in the direction of abstention. This, they stated, should not be allowed to obscure the greater effects of treatment by the treatment centers.[2]

Look again at Table 1 and note that it reveals that almost half (actually 41 percent) of the remissions in the "high treatment" category with no AA participation fell into the so-called normal drinking category. As the discussion section will reveal, despite a lengthy debate, those who endorse the medical model did not raise questions regarding what light the data presented in Table 1 might shed on the abstinence question. With that in mind, the data in Table 1 were collapsed into abstinence and "nonremission and normal drinking" groups. The results are displayed in Table 2.

When abstinence was used as the remission criteria, the data presented in Table 2 presented a very different picture regarding the differential effects of AA and professional treatment.   When the comparison was made between the high treatment and the low-untreated groups without AA participation, the effect of treatment was to increase the abstinence percentage 18 percent, from 24 percent for those in the none-low treatment category to 41 percent for those who received high amounts of treatment. Receipt of treatment had a similar effect on the percentage of abstinence among those who were irregular AA participants, raising the abstinence rate from 27 to 44 percent. For those who regularly attended AA, the remission percentages were 71 and 74 percent. That is, 71 percent of those persons who were in the untreated low treatment category and who regularly attended AA were abstinent while 74 percent of those who received high amounts of treatment and regularly attended AA were abstinent.

When abstinence is used as the remission criteria, the data in Table 2 suggest that those who regularly attend AA had 47 and 32 percent increases in abstinence when compared to the no AA attendance group. Not only do those differences exceed the 18 percent increase in abstinence which can be attributed to treatment, but the data in Table 2 implies that the effect of regular AA attendance is unaffected

Table 2.   Relationship Between Amount of Treatment and Remissions Defined in Terms of Abstinence with Level of AA Attendance Controlled

	Remissions Percentages		
Amount of Treatment	No AA Attendance in Past Year	Irregular AA Attendance	Regular AA Attendance
None/Low Amount Outcome			
Abstained	24	27	71
Drinking	76	73	29
(N)	(268)	(82)	(28)
High Amount Outcome			
Abstained	42	44	74
Drinking	58	56	26
(N)	(112)	(66)	(50)

by the amount of professional treatment received. This interpretation is forthcoming because the difference between 71 and 74 percent is so small as to suggest no effect on abstinence.

Discussion

The reanalysis presented above suggested that the Rand Report (Armor et al., 1978) could have been interpreted as a document favorable to AA. If abstinence is the goal of treatment, then the data related to the differential effectiveness of AA and the treatment delivered by the centers leaves little doubt as to the more effective approach. As suggested above, Armor et al. (1978) clearly indicated AA participation was the major factor associated with abstinence. For those who were supposedly associated with or supporters of that organization, there was little need to reassess the data as has been done here.

AA's supporters did assess and reassess the data. The Rand Report (Armor et al., 1978:232–244) reprinted the transcript of a press conference held by the National Council on Alcoholism which brought together a number of nationally known experts on alcoholism. Collectively, those professionals characterized the study as an attack on alcoholics in general; they universally raised issues regarding the scientific adequacy of the study, especially in terms of the sample size, length of the follow-up period, and what was referred to as the "overly loose" criteria used to construct the normal drinking indicator. AA and its effectiveness in achieving abstinence was not mentioned.

None of the experts present at the press conference challenged the major recommendation forthcoming from the Rand Report (Armor et al., 1978), namely, that the treatment system be retained in its present form. The report had argued that the system be maintained because of its cost effectiveness. It seems that AA's supporters could easily have argued that the treatment system either be abandoned or at least stripped of its professional treatment staff. Since personnel, especially professionals, are the major contributors to costs in social service systems, the cost effectiveness emphasis should have focused attention on AA, which is, after all, a free service. Elsewhere, Moore (1979) argued that many experts press for more AA attendance because it is "so cheap."

Responses of critics to the Rand Report (Armor et al., 1978), and supporters as well, reflect their vested interests in the alcoholism treatment field. AA, per se, had no voice in these proceedings, and no one capitalized on what could have been a major victory for that organization. Referring to the fact that a number of AA members are now employed as paraprofessionals in the formal treatment system, Moore (1979) provided a comment which brings this discussion more into focus. He indicated that professionally staffed programs need the vocal support of AA and that a norm of reciprocity has developed between AA members employed as paraprofessionals and the programs which hire them. He now finds that those given employment no longer hold to the most dogmatic AA positions (like the fact that AA should not be associated with any outside enterprise such as a professional treatment program)[3] but are receptive to psychiatric concepts.

Madsen (1979) responded in a similar vein to the Tournier (1979) article which suggested that AA influence was a roadblock to treatment innovation. To counter that claim, he cited his own study which indicated that AA cooperated with the National Council on Alcoholism and that both organizations were integrated into the local treatment system, making referrals to facilities like hospitals, half-way houses, and other professionally staffed treatment programs.

These comments are consistent with the description of how employment as paraprofessionals is used to co-opt indigenous persons. Earlier, we suggested that it was the organization that will ultimately be the victim of this process. We have described how AA is portrayed in the literature as a major force in social policy related to alcoholism treatment. Nevertheless, the organization, per se, has not been engaged in a single policy debate, and in the case of the Rand Report (Armor et al., 1978), it was theoretically represented by the National Council on Alcoholism.[4] The critique of the Rand Report presented here suggests that AA's supposed ally did not attempt to push for an interpretation of that study which would highlight the effectiveness of AA in achieving abstinence.

The point to be made here is that AA has not had a role in social policy formation related to alcoholism treatment. If the Rand Report (Armor et al., 1978) serves as an example of the loyalty of those who supposedly speak for AA, these more powerful professional persons have done so to protect their own vested interests. We would argue that AA should not be involved in policy issues, and we find that the literature devoted to social movements indicates that cooperation with professionals will ultimately result in co-optation of the organization. AA and its members were denied the recognition that participation in their organization was the major factor in achieving abstinence in the Rand Report. As we have indicated elsewhere (Fry, 1977), that may be a minor loss when the long-term implication of cooperation could be the disintegration of organizational integrity and, finally, loss of control of the organization.

In summary, this paper questioned the notion that certain traditions in social thought on alcoholism result in blaming the individual alcoholic. The argument was made that AA, the organization, has been both hero and villain in the literature and ultimately may become the victim because of its members' relationships with more powerful professional groups. Studies which suggested how indigenous persons and groups are co-opted through their employment as paraprofessionals were cited to bolster that point. A reanalysis of the Rand Report (Armor et al., 1978) data related to the differential effectiveness of AA and professional treatment was presented. The results were interpreted to suggest that AA and its members were denied a major victory concerning that organization's role in obtaining abstinence as a treatment outcome. The conclusion is that there is internal fragmentation in the various traditions (Watts, 1982) identified in social thought related to alcoholism. If self-help groups like AA are to continue to exist as autonomous entities, public policy must encompass the disease approach, which allows alcoholics to assume responsibility for alcoholism without involvement in policy level decisions.

NOTES

1. The interested reader should see Freund, 1981; Madsen, 1979; Roizen, 1978; Sobell and Sobell, 1978.
2. In their four-year follow-up of the original report, Polich et al. (1981:148–152) again reported that abstinence was associated with AA attendance. They presented a table (1981:151) which reflected drinking status at four years by AA attendance at the eighteen-month follow-up. This table revealed that 42 percent of those who were currently attending AA had abstained one year, as compared to 16 percent who had never attended AA. In terms of those who had abstained from the time of the eighteen-month check to the four-year follow-up, 22 percent were currently attending AA regularly while 11 percent of those who never attended AA were abstinent over the same period. However, in their analysis of the factors related to abstinence, AA participation was left out because, they stressed, there was a possibility that

abstainers select themselves to be regular attendees of AA.   It is of interest to note
that they felt free to make comparisons between AA and professional treatment when
they felt free to rely on their "normal drinking" indicator in the earlier report.
3.   Gartner and Reissman (1977:27–28) note that AA is governed by a set of rules
which guide the conduct of AA groups.   The sixth tradition is as follows: An AA
group ought never endorse, finance or lend the AA name to *any* related facility or
outside enterprise, lest problems of money, property and prestige divert us from our
primary purpose.   The preceding tradition, five, reads as follows: Each group has
but one primary purpose—to carry the message to the alcoholic who still suffers.
4.   Earlier, an article was cited by Schneider (1978) in which he attributed the
success of the campaign to gain acceptance of the disease concept to AA, the Yale
Center on Alcohol Studies, and the Jellinek model.   However, Schneider's
description of the events which launched the campaign indicated that AA was not
formally represented.   AA's involvement came from the efforts of a person Schneider
defined as a onetime member of AA who was responsible for the founding of the
National Council on Alcoholism, which, Schneider indicated, she saw as
supplementing the work of AA in public education regarding alcoholism.   This
example provides support for the old belief that AA has not officially or formally
been engaged in policy formulations related to alcoholism treatment.

REFERENCES

Armor, D., J. Polich, and H. Stambul
   1978   *Alcoholism and Treatment*. New York: John Wiley and Sons.
Beauchamp, D.
   1980   *Beyond Alcoholism: Alcohol and Public Health Policy*.   Philadelphia:
      Temple University Press.
Blumberg, L.
   1977   The Ideology of a Therapeutic Social Movement: Alcoholics Anonymous.
      Journal of Studies on Alcohol 38:2122–2143.
Bullington, B., J. Munns, and G. Geis
   1969   Purchase of Conformity: Ex-Narcotics Addicts Among the Bourgeoisie.
      Social Problems 16:456–463.
Cloward, R., and F. Piven
   1974   "The Professional Bureaucracies: Benefit Systems as Influence Systems."
      In *The Politics of Turmoil*, edited by R. Cloward and F. F. Piven, 7–27.
      New York: Pantheon.
Conrad, P., and J. Schneider
   1980   *Deviance and Medicalization: From Badness to Sickness*. St. Louis: C. V.
      Mosby.
Freund, P.
   1976   The Impact of Formal Inmate Structure on Opposition to Staff and
      Treatment Goals. *British Journal of Criminology* 16:126–141.

Freund, P.
1981 Review of Alcoholism and Treatment. *Contemporary Sociology* 10: (March): 284–285.
Fry, L.
1977 Research Grants and Drug Self-Help Programs: What Price Knowledge? *Journal of Health and Social Behavior* 18:405–417.
Gartner, A., and F. Reissman
1977 *Self-Help in the Human Services.* San Francisco: Jossey-Bass.
Gurr, T.
1970 *Why Men Rebel.* Princeton, N.J.: Princeton University Press.
Madsen, W.
1979 Comment on Tournier. *Journal of Studies on Alcohol* 40:323–328.
McCarthy, J., and M. Zald
1977 Resource Mobilization in Social Movements: A Partial Theory. *American Journal of Sociology* 82:1212–1239.
Moore, R.
1979 Comment on Tournier. *Journal of Studies on Alcohol* 40:328–330.
Oberschall, A.
1973 *Social Conflict and Social Movements.* Englewood Cliffs, N.J.: Prentice-Hall.
Pattison, E., M. Sobell, and L. Sobell
1977 *Emerging Concepts of Alcohol Dependence.* New York: Springer Press.
Piven, J.
1974 "The New Urban Programs; The Strategy of Federal Intervention." In *The Politics of Turmoil,* edited by R. Cloward and F. Piven, 284–313. New York: Pantheon.
Polich, J., D. Armor, and H. Braiker
1981 *The Course of Alcoholism: Four Years After Treatment.* New York: John Wiley & Sons.
Reissman, F.
1965 The Helper Therapy Principle. *Social Work* 10:27–32.
Roizen, R.
1978 "Comment Rand Report." In *Alcoholism and Treatment,* edited by D. Armor, J. Polich, and H. Stambul, 265–275. New York: John Wiley & Sons.
Schneider, J.
1978 Deviant Drinking as Disease: Alcoholism as a Social Accomplishment. *Social Problems* 25 (April): 361–372.
Smelser, N.
1969 *Theory of Collective Behavior.* New York: Free Press.
Sobell, M., and L. Sobell
1979 Comment on Tournier. *Journal of Studies on Alcohol* 40:320–322.
Tournier, R.
1979 Alcoholics Anonymous as Treatment and as Ideology. *Journal of Studies on Alcohol* 40:230–239.

Turner, R., and L. Killian
   1972   *Collective Behavior.* Englewood Cliffs, N.J.: Prentice-Hall.
Watts, T.
   1982   Three Traditions in Social Thought on Alcoholism.   *International Journal of Addictions* 17:1231–1239.
Wilson, J.
   1973   *Introduction to Social Movements.* New York: Basic Books.

INDEX

Advertising, of alcohol, 71–72
Alcoholics Anonymous (AA)
  as concept for alcoholic treatment,
  10–12
  comparison with other concepts, 23
  focus on "way of life," 123–27
  method for changing social thought,
  117–18
  outgrowth of Prohibition failure, 61
  religious approach, 53, 55, 64
  research findings on, 127–29
Alcoholism, theoretical approaches
  Alcoholics Anonymous, 10–12
  behavioral, 17–19, 43–47
  family interaction, 16–17
  medical (disease), 14–15, 25–26,
  30–31, 39–46, 48–50, 73, 124
  psychoanalytic, 12–14
  social psychological (addiction),
  27–35, 43–47
  sociological, 19–21
  transactional analysis, 21–23
Americans, beliefs about alcohol,
  67–75

"Battle Hymn of the Republic," 121,
  129n.3
Bible, on use of alcohol, 53, 55–56
Black Americans, alcohol and drug use,
  3–4, 111

Calvinism, 58–59, 118–19, 121,
  129n.2

Drug use, 53, 104n.5, 105n.9, 109–15

Ego Mafia, 32, 35n.3

Greeting cards, alcohol themes in,
  71–72

Hammett, Dashiell, 35
Harris, L., public opinion poll,
  111–15
Hellman, Lillian, 35
Hispanic Americans, and alcohol, 3

Jellinek, E. M., 25, 40–41, 61, 109,
  121, 123, 124, 139, 149n.4

Kovel, Joel, 32, 33, 35n.2

Levine, H. G., 70, 129n.2

MacAndrew and Edgerton, studies of,
  67, 69, 72, 73, 74
McClelland, David, 25, 31–32
McCook, John James, social reformer
  background, 90–92, 104n.1
  photographic and social
  investigations, 92–99, 104nn.2,3
  proposed solutions, 101–3,
  105nn.7,8
  thoughts and views on alcoholism,
  99–101, 104nn.4,5, 105n.6
  views on drugs, 104n.5, 105n.9
Marijuana use. *See also* Drug use
  link with alcohol, 109–15
  medical versus public health
  problem, 109–15
  public opinion on, 111–15

Narcotics. *See* Drug use, Marijuana
  use.
National Council on Alcoholism, 41,
  61, 140, 146, 147, 149n.4
Native Americans, and alcohol, 3, 63,
  80, 119